THE BATTLE OF LANSDOWN

1643

Other books by John Wroughton:

Tudor Bath: Life and Strife in the Little City, 1485-1603 (2006)

The Routledge Companion to the Stuart Age, 1603-1714 (2006)

Stuart Bath: Life in the Forgotten City, 1603-1714 (2004)

450 Years: King Edward's School, Bath, 1552-2002 (2002)

Mr Colston's Hospital: The History of Colston's School, Bristol (2002)

An Unhappy Civil War (1999)

The Stuart Age, 1603-1714 (1997)

A Community at War: the Civil War in Bath and North Somerset (1992)

King Edward's School at Bath, 1552-1982 (1982)

English Historical Facts, 1603-1688 (with Chris Cook, 1980)

Seventeenth-Century Britain (1980)

Documents on World History (2 vols., with Denys Cook, 1976)

Bath in the Age of Reform, 1830-41 (1972)

Documents on British Political History (3 vols., 1971)

Smuggling (with John Paxton, 1971)

Plots, Traitors and Spies, 1653-85 (1970)

Cromwell and the Roundheads (1969)

THE

BATTLE OF LANSDOWN

1643

AN EXPLORER'S GUIDE

JOHN WROUGHTON

with Line Drawings by Stephen Beck
and Original Paintings by Shane Feeney

*Thus stood the two armies taking breath looking upon each other, our cannon on both sides
playing without ceasing till it was dark - legs and arms flying apace.*
(Walter Slingsby, royalist colonel of infantry)

*We had a weary and dangerous day's fight, the night parting us; and so well did we knock
each other about that, in the night, we both retreated.*
(Sir William Waller, commander of the parliamentarian army)

THE LANSDOWN PRESS

First published in 2008 by
The Lansdown Press
41 The Empire   Grand Parade
Bath BA2 4DF

ISBN 978-0-9520249-8-9

Typeset in 11 / 13 Times New Roman
Typesetting and design by
The Lansdown Press, Bath

Printed in Great Britain by
Cpod, Trowbridge, Wiltshire

Contents

Introduction

When I arrived in Bath in 1965, it quickly became apparent from its recorded history that the city's 'Dark Age' was much more extensive than elsewhere, stretching as it did from the end of the Roman occupation right through to the eighteenth century. This shameful neglect of its heritage over many years (even though the city's archives were actually bursting with undiscovered information) meant that vital moments in its past lay shrouded in mist.

My hope is that the four books published since 1992 (*Tudor Bath, 1485-1603; Stuart Bath, 1603-1714; A Community at War: the Civil War in Bath and North-East Somerset, 1642-50;* and this present volume) will help in some small measure to fill that gap - at least as far as the sixteenth and seventeenth centuries are concerned.

In *The Battle of Lansdown* I have attempted not only to provide a background to the battle and to describe the action in all its exciting detail, but also to take the reader on an exploration of both the battlefield and the surviving eye-witness accounts. Maps are also provided of two walks to encourage further individual investigation. A.L. Rouse's old advice to would-be historians is still relevant today: 'The first thing you must do', he wrote, 'is to go out and buy yourself a strong pair of boots'. This is particularly important when studying a battle such as this, where the nature of the terrain was so crucial to tactics and the deployment of troops. Sadly, some modern historians have attempted to write about the action on Lansdown without ever visiting the site - with predictable consequences!

John Wroughton

Acknowledgments

The author wishes to thank the many people who have contributed to the production of this book. These include those who have helped to provide illustrations - Shane Feeney for his superb original paintings, which also appear on the interpretation panels on the Lansdown battlefield; Pat Beck for permission to use her late husband's imaginative line drawings, which I commissioned for my previous books; Stephen Bird, Head of Heritage Services in Bath; James Methuen-Campbell of Corsham Court; the Courtauld Institute of Art; the Royal Armouries Museum, Leeds; the National Archives, London; the National Portrait Gallery, London; the Ashmolean Museum, Oxford; P J N Prideaux-Brune of Prideaux Place; Mike Chapman for the maps of the battle area; Paul Davis; Ruth Skrine; P J Sheeman; the Governors of King Edward's School, Bath; and Osprey Publishing Ltd for two images from their Elite Series 25, *Soldiers of the English Civil War 1: Infantry* by Keith Roberts and Angus McBride.

Others who have assisted at various points in the book's production are Martin Latham for his striking cover design; Paul Lamb of Cpod, the printers, for his patient and practical advice; the staff of Bath Record Office, the Bodleian Library, the British Library and the National Archives for their expertise in my search for documentary material; and Marek Lewcun for his help over archaeological detail.

Chronology of the Local War

Major national events and battles are shown in italics; local events in plain type

1642

5 Aug: Rally of 12,000 people at Chewton Mendip in support of parliament. North-East Somerset firmly under parliamentarian control.

22 Aug: King raises standard at Nottingham to signify the official start of war.

23 Oct: Battle of Edgehill, near Kineton, Warwickshire.

1643

19 Jan: Battle of Braddock Down, Cornwall.

30 June: Battle of Adwalton Moor, near Bradford, Yorkshire.

5 July: Battle of Lansdown, near Bath.

13 July: Battle of Roundway Down, near Devizes, Wiltshire. Bath is taken by the royalists a few days later.

26 July: Surrender of Bristol to the royalists after a short siege. The West is now largely under royalist control.

10 Aug: Siege of Gloucester begins, but remains in parliamentarian hands.

20 Sept: First Battle of Newbury, Berkshire.

1644

29 Mar: Battle of Cheriton, Hampshire.

29 June: Battle of Cropredy Bridge, Oxfordshire.

2 July: Battle of Marston Moor, near York.

27 Oct: Second Battle of Newbury, Berkshire.

1645

14 June: Battle of Naseby, Northamptonshire.

10 July: Battle of Langport, Somerset.

30 July: Bath, garrisoned by royalists under Sir Thomas Bridges of Keynsham, surrenders to a detachment of parliament's New Model Army under Colonel Rich .

20 Aug: Capture of Nunney Castle by a detachment of the New Model Army under Colonel Thomas Rainsborough.

23 August: Siege of Bristol begins by the New Model Army.

4 Sept: A rally of 5000 local people in support of the New Model Army is addressed by Oliver Cromwell at Chewton Mendip.

10 Sept: Prince Rupert surrenders Bristol to General Thomas Fairfax.

15 Sept: Farleigh Castle recaptured by its owner, Sir Edward Hungerford (a parliamentarian) from his own half-brother, Sir John Hungerford (a royalist).

1646

16 Feb: Battle of Torrington, Devon; the king's western army is defeated.

21 Mar: The remaining royalist field force surrenders at Stow-on-the Wold.

5 May: Charles I surrenders to the Scots at Southwell, Nottinghamshire.

29 May: Bath's garrison is finally withdrawn; city council is given permission to dismantle fortifications.

1

Exploring the Evidence

The Landscape

Those wishing to explore the Battle of Lansdown are extremely fortunate in two respects. In the first place, the battlefield itself has changed remarkably little since the time of the battle in 1643. An investigation by English Heritage for the Battlefields Register in 1995 concluded that the seventeenth-century landscape 'was substantially the same as that apparent today'. Therefore most of the present-day hedges, stone walls, woods and roads (all of which are mentioned in contemporary accounts) combine to give a good impression of the very landscape which the armies encountered - even though the woodland has expanded on the northern slopes of the down while enclosures have multiplied on its flat top.

Even more exciting is the fact that several features which played a crucial part in the latter stages of the battle (including 'Waller's Wall', the old quarry pits and the Roman earthworks) are - as we shall see - clearly evident today. These act as a great spur to the imagination as the story of the battle unfolds - as does the dramatic view gained from Hanging Hill of the difficult terrain over which the royalist army advanced from Tog Hill and Freezing Hill before dropping down into the valley below. This was the same view that Waller's parliamentarian army had of the enemy force from its earthworks on the northern ridge of the down. Standing on this spot today, we can quickly grasp the major impact of the terrain on the nature of the battle and the daunting task facing the royalists as they launched an assault on such a steep escarpment from some 225 feet below.

All these features are clearly visible from public roads and footpaths, including the Cotswold Way (which boasts easily-accessible and well-maintained stiles). Furthermore, four battlefield interpretation panels were erected in 2003 together with ten orange banners along the Cotswold Way, which mark out the extent of the battlefield .

Freezing Hill with Tog Hill in the distance - the view from Hanging Hill of the line of the royalists' advance. (Author's collection)

Written Sources

We are also fortunate in having a number of vivid eyewitness accounts of the battle, which help us to pinpoint exactly where much of the action took place. From the royalist perspective, these include the personal account of the western campaign by **Sir Ralph Hopton** (the Field Marshal General) - a campaign in which he played a leading part. This was written during his exile in Jersey in 1646 to assist the Earl of Clarendon, who was compiling his *History of the Great Rebellion*. The same motivation also prompted the account written by **Colonel Walter Slingsby** (royalist colonel of infantry), which was completed in 1647. His narrative, which displays a dry sense of humour, is remarkably balanced and fair in its judgements. Whereas both these memoirs were finished within four years of the battle, while memories were still fresh, the version left by **Captain Richard Atkyns** (a captain in Prince Maurice's regiment of horse, who was promoted to major at the end of the conflict) was not completed until 1669. Although he does manage to convey something of the atmosphere of the battle, his version is not totally reliable in detail - and it was actually written as a justification of his life while in prison for debt.

The parliamentarian sources are less substantial. A letter by one of its cavalry captains (**Edward Harley**) to his father just ten days after the battle is valuable in describing clearly what happened, while the parliamentarian tract *A True Relation of the Great and Glorious Victory* (published in July 1643) provides some vivid detail. **Sir William Waller's** despatch to the Speaker of the Commons (12 July 1643) adds a number of additional points to the story. **Tracts and news-sheets**, which proliferated during the war period, were systematically collected by a London bookseller (George Thomason) and are now available in the British Library. Although rich in colour, they are inevitably prone to bias and need therefore to be treated with caution. Parliamentarian news-sheets employed here include *A Perfect Diurnal* (10-17 July 1643) and *Special Passages* (19 July 1643), whereas the most relevant royalist one is *Mercurius Aulicus* (8 July 1643).

Two publications, which were written by men who were not present at the battle and which therefore relied on material supplied by others, are *Jehovah Jireh* by **John Vicars** (an ardent puritan and supporter of parliament), whose first volume containing an account of the battle was published in 1644; and Edward Hyde, **1st Earl of Clarendon** (a faithful servant of both Charles I and Charles II), whose *History of the Great Rebellion* was started during his first exile in Jersey in 1646 and completed during his second exile in France in 1667. Whereas Vicars tends to be highly prejudiced, Clarendon is much more balanced in his judgements.

From these sources and the landscape itself, it is possible to trace out both the extent of the battlefield and the progress of the battle. Full details of the source material mentioned above can be found in the bibliography. **Archaeology and local legend** also have a part to play in reconstructing the past as a study of this battlefield will reveal.

The Nation's Drift to War

The Issues at Stake

Charles I, who succeeded James I as King of England, Scotland and Ireland in 1625, quickly became embroiled in a series of bitter clashes with parliament over religion, foreign policy and taxation. This simmering dispute finally erupted into a major crisis in 1629, when the House of Commons passed The Three Resolutions based on their major grievances - with the Speaker forcibly held down in the Chair! In a fury, the king dissolved parliament and launched a period of 'personal rule' (1629-40). His popularity rapidly plummeted.

King Charles I (author's collection)

Believing in the Divine Right of Kings (i.e. that his right to govern came from God and not from the people), he proceeded to rule without parliament, raising a series of 'illegal' taxes and imposing High Church practices in religion through his Archbishop, William Laud.

Opponents who wrote pamphlets attacking these changes in religion were subjected to the harshest punishment. William Prynne of Swainswick (near Bath), for instance, was condemned to suffer not only a heavy fine, a spell in the stocks and imprisonment for life, but also the cutting off of his ears and the branding of both cheeks with the letters 'S L' ('seditious libeller'). It is hardly surprising, therefore, that Prynne was to emerge as one of the chief supporters of parliament in North-East Somerset when the Civil War broke out in 1642.

Meanwhile, civil war had already erupted in Scotland in protest at the king's attempt to impose his unpopular religious policies there. Fierce rioting quickly led to war - and it was this war in Scotland (together with another rebellion in Ireland) that eventually forced Charles to recall parliament in 1640. The fact was that he urgently needed large amounts of cash to finance an army

*Above - William Prynne of Swainswick ,
later MP for Bath.
(By courtesy of King Edward's School, Bath).
Below - John Pym, one of the five MPs arrested.
(Author's collection)*

for the suppression of these troublemakers. His opponents quickly seized their opportunity to demand - in return for these much-needed taxes - the reform of current abuses and a guarantee over future policy.

Two matters were of particular concern. The Protestants (many of whom were devout Puritans, believing in the importance of scripture) feared that Charles, whose wife (Queen Henrietta Maria) was a practising Catholic, would ally with Spain and impose catholicism on the country by force. Others feared that the constitution was being undermined and were determined to ensure that parliament played a much more regular and active part in the government of the country.

The Beginning of Conflict

These concerns were summarised in the Grand Remonstrance of November 1641. This move so incensed Charles that, on 5 January 1642, he entered the Commons with an escort of troops and attempted to arrest his five leading critics. These included John Pym (a Somerset man) and Sir Arthur Haselrig (who later fought for parliament at Lansdown in 1643). This intrusion was a violation of parliamentary freedom and privilege. There was uproar on the streets of London as rumours circulated about the king's intentions. The local trained bands were therefore quickly mustered to defend themselves and their property against attack. The king, realising that he had now lost control, fled his capital with forty retainers and headed for York. The drift to civil war had begun - a war which few had predicted and few really wanted. Sadly, however, Charles I - a stubborn and inflexible character - was incapable of compromise.

Civil War was officially declared when Charles raised his standard at Nottingham on 22 August 1642. In general it is true to say that much of the south and east of the country, including

London and all the major ports, declared for parliament; while most of the north and the west remained loyal to the king. In reality, however, each county, each town and each village was divided by the war (and even some families), while many tried hard to remain neutral. Nor was it a 'total' war in the modern sense with the whole civilian population targeted and involved, but essentially a war between two campaigning armies. Out of a parliament of six hundred and fifty members (including five hundred in the Commons), just three hundred or so actively supported war against the king - inspired no doubt by the fervent speeches of John Pym and the excellence of his planning.

A contemporary print showing the raising of the king's standard outside Nottingham Castle, 22 August 1642. (Author's collection)

Bath as a Garrison Town in 1642

The City Braces itself for War

When the Civil War broke out in 1642, Bath was still a compact medieval city, housing no more than two thousand people. The vast majority of these lived in houses protected by a well-maintained medieval city wall and flanking ditch, which were themselves surrounded by fields and orchards. The four main gateways to the city, which were locked at night, were strongly fortified and were further strengthened during the Civil War by earthworks and barricades. The river Avon, of course, which looped round the city, gave a further measure of protection on three sides. The only bridge over the river, situated at the bottom of Southgate Street, was also protected by its own gate, while Gascoyn's Tower in the north-western corner of the city provided a raised platform for heavy artillery.

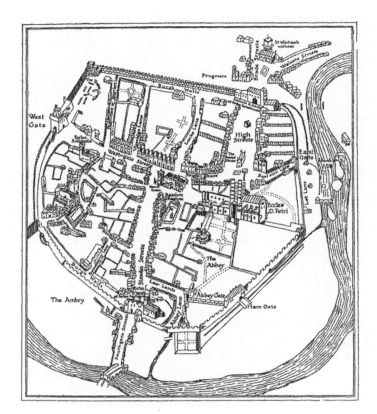

Based on John Speed's late sixteenth-century map of Bath, showing the medieval walls and gates. (Author's collection)

The city was governed by a mayor and corporation, consisting of ten aldermen and twenty common councillors, who between them were responsible for electing two members of parliament. They took great pride in their fine facilities, which included four 'hospitals' or almshouses, a handsome new guildhall, a lively market place, a grammar school and three active churches, including the city's splendid new parish church (later to be styled Bath Abbey). Furthermore, an old redundant church was used to house the town prison in its tower and the grammar school in its nave.

The busy North Gate standing next to the disused church of St Mary, which housed both the school and the prison. A line drawing by Stephen Beck.

In the months before hostilities commenced, the city council - sensing that times were becoming dangerous - set about the task of preparing for war (against persons at that stage unknown!). Old muskets were repaired in the guildhall armoury, to which were added new stocks of gunpowder, bullets, pikes and armour. Holes in the city walls were patched, locks on the gates replaced and the surrounding ditch scoured. To improve night-time security, three teams of guards were established to patrol the streets at regular intervals, thus supplementing the work of the bellman and two watchmen whose normal task was to look out for fire, felon or intruder.

The City's Advantages in War

Bath actually had many advantages when it came to war. It was a wealthy city with affluence based on the cloth industry, agriculture and   health tourism (centred around its hot water baths). The latter continued to flourish throughout the war as wounded soldiers flocked to the city to gain a cure - thus replacing those normal clients from the court, who had fled with the king to York. Crowds of visitors therefore provided a lucrative trade for the inns, shops and lodging houses. The fine stone buildings, which had been built in Tudor times, were testimony to the city's on-going prosperity. This meant that, in spite of heavy expenditure on the war effort, the council - unlike those in most other cities - always had money in hand at the end of every financial year.

It was also a healthy city because, unlike Bristol, it did not rely on the polluted waters of the river during times of drought or siege. Fresh water from springs on neighbouring hills, piped down into the city, supplied both private houses and public drinking fountains. Its reputation as a largely disease-free city meant that royalty (including the king and the queen) and high-ranking officers (including both Cromwell and Fairfax) stayed in Bath rather than Bristol during visits to the area.

During 1642-43, Bath City Council spent heavily on defence, as illustrated by these extracts from the Bath Chamberlain's Accounts.

Roger Browne for work done on the Bridge Gate..............................	*00 18 00*
For raising the city wall at James churchyard................................	*00 12 00*
For wood, coal and candles for 3 courts of guard............................	*03 10 08*
Jellicotts for work and iron about the carriages of the great guns....	*00 15 06*
Captain Clift for keys and mending the locks of the city gates.........	*00 02 10*
For carrying up of arms into the Hall..	*00 02 00*
For removing of the great guns from the Mount...............................	*00 05 00*
For walling up the gates and the doors about the city wall..............	*00 08 00*
For making a sentry house and for mending the prison....................	*00 11 00*
For placing the barrels of match in the Hall..................................	*00 01 00*
For two old barrels to hold the bullets in..	*00 01 00*
For setting up and taking down barricades at East and West Gates.	*00 08 06*
For a drum for the city use...	*02 00 00*

By Stephen Beck

4

Bath's Day of Decision, July 1642

Religion - the Main Local Issue

The community of Bath and North-East Somerset was greatly influenced in its attitude to the impending war by a number of leading gentry and clothiers. These included Alexander Popham of Hunstrete, Sir John Horner of Mells, Sir Edward Hungerford of Farleigh, John Harington of Kelston, William Prynne of Swainswick and John Ashe of Freshford. All of these were deeply puritan in religion and one of them, William Prynne, had twice been imprisoned in the Tower of London during the 1630s for writing pamphlets against the court and the bishops. Although taxation was a cause for discontent among clothiers like Ashe, religion was undoubtedly the main driving force when the area rose up to support parliament.

During the first thirty years of the seventeenth century, a puritan revolution had swept through North Somerset, bringing about the introduction of mid-week religious lectures; the closing down of many alehouses; the suppression of fairs, bear-baitings and plays; the banning of unlawful games, swearing and sabbath breaking; the removal of maypoles and the tightening of moral standards. However, in a counter-attack during the 1630s, led by William Piers, Bishop of Bath and Wells and an ally of Archbishop Laud, jollifications at parish feasts were restored, midweek lectures banned and High Church practices re-introduced into local parishes - much to the fury of the Puritans.

John Ashe, clothier of Freshford. Portrait by Sir Peter Lely (1618-80). By courtesy of the Methuen Collection, Corsham Court. Photograph: Photographic Survey, Courtauld Institute of Art.

The Situation Erupts

The situation was therefore ripe for conflict. Consequently, when the Marquis of Hertford arrived in Bath in July 1642 with a commission of array from the king to raise the area for the royalist cause, local people feared that the Catholics were upon them - and that Hertford's secret task was to impose catholicism on the area by force. As Richard Baxter wrote at the time: 'Civil war had begun in our streets before king and parliament had any armies'. Whatever the situation elsewhere in the country, the Civil War - in Bath and North-East Somerset at least - was to become a war of religion.

William Seymour, 1st Marquis of Hertford. A drawing by W.N. Gardiner from a portrait by Van Dyke. By courtesy of the Ashmolean Museum, University of Oxford. Photograph: Photographic Survey, Courtauld Institute of Art.

Hertford, finding his reception on the streets of Bath none too friendly, decided to base himself in Wells under the wing of the bishop. Whereupon local parliamentarian leaders, on 5 August, quickly organised a mass rally of some twelve thousand poorly-armed supporters at Chewton Mendip (including the Bath Regiment of trained bands and many others from Bath), before finally pitching camp on the hills overlooking Wells. There, after receiving cartloads of food sent in by neighbouring villages, they spent the night in prayer and the singing of psalms. Next day, this ragtag army began a light bombardment of the city below, aiming shots particularly on the Bishop's Palace. Hertford - many of whose nine hundred supporters had fled up the hill overnight to join their friends in the other camp - wisely decided to make his escape from the county.

A Divided Local Community

In spite of this upsurge of support for parliament in North-East Somerset, the Civil War - like all civil wars - was to tear communities apart. On the city council in Bath, the seven or eight royalist adherents were heavily outnumbered by the firm supporters of parliament - although a further group remained moderate or neutral in its beliefs. But although the councillors were deeply divided politically, only a few of them actually fought on the field of battle. The rest continued to sit side-by-side throughout the hostilities. They were after all friends, neighbours and relatives, whose top priority was to maintain the flow of everyday life in the city. After all, their very livelihood was at stake.

In Somerset, the county was largely parliamentarian in sympathy in the north and royalist in the south - but only five out of its sixteen members of parliament actively fought against the king when it came to war. Furthermore, of the two MPs who represented Bath in 1642, one (Alexander Popham) supported parliament, while the other (Sir William Bassett) supported the king - the latter after a great crisis of confidence.

Locally, as elsewhere, families and neighbours were torn apart. The influential Chapman family, which dominated Bath council, was split down the middle. But it was even more heart-rending for Sir Edward Hungerford when he captured Farleigh Castle in 1645, for he took it from his own half-brother, Sir John, who was a royalist. Much more devastating still was the situation at Wardour Castle when it was stormed by royalists in 1644. One of their musketeers (a man named Hillsdean) was shot dead by his own brother, who was a member of the parliamentarian garrison. Human anguish of this kind was to be experienced in almost every village. For instance, when the pro-royalist lord of the manor of Claverton (Sir William Bassett) attended the little church next door, he found himself listening to the rector (Humphrey Chambers) who was a firebrand puritan and an ardent supporter of parliament.

The Bath Regiment in camp on the Mendips with tents supplied by Bath Council. Notice the women who are helping with food and washing - and the cart of supplies sent in from a neighbouring village. Line drawing by Stephen Beck.

5

The Bath Regiment of Trained Bands

The Trained Bands System

When the Civil War broke out in England in August 1642, ordinary people in North-East Somerset were quickly caught up in front-line action. Indeed, there were already some citizens in Bath who could be classed as 'trained soldiers'. Although the country did not as yet possess a professional standing army, the city of London and a few counties (includ12ing Somerset) still maintained the system of 'trained bands' on which Elizabeth I had based the country's defences from 1573 in anticipation of a Spanish invasion. The system was financed by a trained-soldiers' rate imposed on each parish (to cover the cost of equipment and routine expenses) and controlled by the deputy lieutenants, who checked on the quality of training at annual musters. The purpose was to provide an effective home guard, which would defend the county in time of invasion or local uprising. As such, the trained bands were not expected to operate beyond their county boundary.

They were usually commanded and trained by younger members of the gentry, who were themselves totally inexperienced in warfare (although some of the corporals were old soldiers who had returned from continental campaigns). One of the exceptions in North Somerset was Sir Ralph Hopton of Witham Friary, who had served as a volunteer in the Thirty Years' War.

The Trained Bands on parade in 1642. (A line drawing by Stephen Beck).

The highlight of the year for the trained bands was undoubtedly the annual regimental muster in the summer, when more detailed training in tactics could be given. In practice, the musters were often undermined by large-scale absenteeism as a result of their clash with the harvest - even though absentees risked a fine of forty shillings or ten days in gaol. To compensate for the sacrifice of time, members of the Somerset trained bands were paid eight pence per day for the muster weekend - a most generous rate, when compared with labourers' wages at the time (often no more than one-and-a-half pence a day).

By 1638, the Somerset trained bands (or county militia) numbered 4,000 foot (including 2,403 musketeers and 1597 pikemen) and 300 horse (made up of 82 heavily-armoured cuirassiers and 218 lightly-armoured harquebusiers). The infantry was organised into five regiments, including the Bath Regiment. Each regiment consisted of seven companies - but in order to produce something of a local spirit, each company was recruited from a group of neighbouring parishes. The regiment of cavalry was recruited and equipped largely from the gentry class.

The Bath Regiment in Peace

From a muster roll dated in Bath on 22nd May 1639, we know that the Bath Regiment, commanded at the time by Sir Ralph Hopton, was drawn from the north-eastern part of the county. The infantrymen were selected from all the local parishes, each with its own allocation ranging from eight for the town of Keynsham to just one for the villages of Widcombe, Nunney and North Stoke. Bath itself contributed between twenty and thirty men, whose arms were provided by the city. Parish constables were responsible for ensuring that individual quotas were maintained.

The local Bath company met for training in the city once a month, setting up targets for shooting practice on banks of turf or 'butts' in a close known as 'Butt Haies' and drilling in a meadow outside the West Gate. Their weapons were stored and maintained in the Guildhall, where John Gray, the armourer, was given periodic payments for such tasks as 'scouring the armour', 'mending the faults in the armoury' or 'a board to set the armour on'.

Target practice for Trained Band musketeers outside Bath Abbey. Line drawing by Stephen Beck.

The armoury in the Guildhall where the weapons and armour of the Bath Regiment of Trained bands were stored. (Line drawing by Stephen Beck).

Once a year, the seven companies of whole Bath Regiment joined together for their grand two-day muster. Until the late 1630s, this normally took place in Bath itself. In 1635, for instance, the council authorised the colonel to muster his men on the town common and erect a tent for the officers. Then, while the inspecting officers (i.e. the deputy lieutenants of the county) were entertained to a splendid dinner in the Guildhall, the council provided a large barrel of beer and a good supply of ale for the men to enjoy.

However, by the time of the Civil War, the musters had been moved to Wells, where they were attended by all the regiments in the Somerset force. The Bath Regiment was generously supported there by the Bath Corporation. In 1642, for instance, it contributed a sum of £4 18s 4d towards the constables' expenses in escorting the soldiers to Wells and hiring horses. At the same time, it sent all the arms from its armoury, paying Thomas Saunders to transport them down to Wells. Furthermore, one of its own members was despatched with a large supply of wine to entertain the colonel and other officers at a total cost of £6 17s 9d (no mean sum at the time).

The Regiment in War

During peacetime, membership of the trained bands could often provide a pleasurable pastime - a largely voluntary activity, which also provided a degree of social recognition. The outbreak of hostilities in 1642, however, quickly brought members of the Bath Trained Bands face-to-face with the stark realities of war. By September, at the siege of Sherborne, they had tasted the sheer horror of conflict. According to an eye-witness, they ran 'as if the devil had been in them...when they heard the bullets whistle about their ears'. Over half the 3,000 foot soldiers present deserted in terror!

Once the Civil War had started in earnest, both king and parliament - faced with the urgent task of creating armies from scratch - made a dash to control those few trained bands which were still in operation (including the ones in Somerset). Both sides therefore turned to groups of influential supporters in each area to raise the local bands on their behalf - the king through the issue of commissions of array and parliament through the establishment of county committees. The struggle for control of Somerset was quickly won by parliament (see page 10). By this time, command of the Bath Regiment had passed from Sir Ralph Hopton to Colonel Alexander Popham (two men who would find themselves on opposing sides in the Lansdown campaign).

However, parliament soon realised that these poorly-equipped troops alone would be insufficient to win the war. From the summer of 1642, therefore, it began to call for voluntary donations of money and weapons for the parliamentary cause, organised by the local committee and collected at the Guildhall in Bath. Assistant collectors were appointed to visit 'people of ability' and persuade them to subscribe. The response was most encouraging. In Keynsham, for instance, forty people lent between them a total of £82 15s 0d. Individual donations varied between five shillings and ten pounds, some of them in the form of plate. A further twenty-eight people combined to provide eighteen horses (most of them fully equipped), twenty-two muskets, eighteen swords, eleven bandoliers, four pistols, five pikes, one halberd, one 'birding piece' and a 'new corslet and head piece' at a total cost of £133 2s 8d.

The aim of this fundraising was to equip a new regiment of dragoons under Colonel Alexander Popham who, from January 1643, became commander of a much-enlarged Bath Regiment (built on the

Alexander Popham, MP for Bath and commander of the Bath Regiment. (By courtesy of the Board of Trustees of the Royal Armouries, accession no. I.315).

foundations of the old trained bands). For it was at this moment that parliament began in earnest to encourage the recruitment of volunteers to boost the old force. Many responded. John Ashe, the great clothier from Freshford, for instance 'raised, armed and for many weeks paid a troop of horse, a company of foot and a company of dragoons for the service of the west country...and paid for powder, match and bullet expended by them all, which cost him above £3,000'.

Popham's new regiment (with a nominal strength of 2000 men) was to see a great deal of active service in 1643. Although based in Bristol as part of that city's garrison, it took part in the successful capture of Sherborne in April; skirmishes around Frome and Norton St Philip in May; and a bloody action around Glastonbury and the Mendips in June as parliamentarian forces attempted to halt the advance of the royalist army under Sir Ralph Hopton. It was not released by the Bristol garrison to assist Sir William Waller at Lansdown until the actual day of the battle, although afterwards it did accompany him to Devizes in pursuit of Hopton's bedraggled army. It was there, however, at the Battle of Roundway Down, that the Bath Regiment was largely destroyed with the rest of Waller's force.

An extract from the Somerset Assessments, 1642, listing some of the voluntary contributions made in Keynsham to equip troops on behalf of parliament.

(By courtesy of the National Archives, SP28.175)

6

Civil War Armies

Recruitment

As there were no ready-made armies in 1642, both king and parliament initially scrambled to enlist the services of the local trained bands. These inexperienced forces were supplemented from January 1643 by regiments and troops of volunteers, raised and funded by members of the local nobility and gentry. Although from late 1643 - as the supply of volunteers dried up - each side adopted a form of conscription, armies were notoriously unreliable and subject to mutiny or desertion until the establishment of parliament's professional New Model Army in 1645.

Conditions

The 'marching armies' could be expected to march at least twenty miles a day and around one thousand miles in a year - often over difficult terrain. In theory, a soldier's daily ration consisted of bread or biscuit, cheese and salted meat, carried in his 'snapsack' (or backpack). A properly organised commissariat for the armies, however, was not in place until 1644. In practice, therefore, supplies were irregular with individuals being forced to fend for themselves and often exhausted through lack of sustenance.

A recruiting officer at work in 1643. (An original painting by Angus McBride - by courtesy of © Osprey Publishing Ltd.)

Quartermasters tried where possible to arrange billets with inhabitants of towns and villages along the route, but accommodation was limited and the country population impoverished with little to spare. Soldiers therefore resorted to plundering farm produce or gaining official requisition orders from officers, thus enabling them to 'live off the

A company of pikemen on the march. A woodcut by permission of the British Library (Roxburghe Ballads, RAX.II, 56).

country'. Henry Foster, returning to London from Gloucester in 1643 with the trained bands, recorded that the army drove along one thousand requisitioned sheep and sixty cattle - with eighty-seven sheep allocated to his own regiment.

Nor could the troops afford to buy food in the markets - for although in theory the trained bands were paid eight pence a day, payments were irregular and heavily in arrears with large deductions made for upkeep. Members of the trained bands (if lucky) would have been issued with coats, shoes, shirts, caps and snapsacks, but the clothing was often poor in quality and quickly wore out.

Composition of Armies

The ideal civil war army would consist of infantry (two-thirds) and cavalry (one-third). The infantry was organised into regiments, each totalling 1200 men divided into ten companies and commanded by a colonel. Each company consisted of musketeers (two-thirds) and pikemen (one-third). The cavalry regiment, again commanded by a colonel, was composed of six troops of 60 (later 100) men each. The army would also contain the artillery and a small number of dragoons or mounted infantry for special assignments.

Musketeers

At the start of the war, the musketeer carried a matchlock musket with a four-foot barrel; a lintock or musket rest; a smoldering length of cord or 'match'; a flask of fine powder with which to prime the flash-pan; a leather baldrick across the chest from which hung a bullet bag; a scouring stick (or ramrod) and twelve bandoliers (or small tube-like cases made of tin, leather or wood), each containing a charge of powder; and a sword. Sometimes the musketeer carried a supply of powder made up into paper cartridges instead of the bandoliers. He normally wore a buff [leather] coat and a soft hat, but no metal armour.

In battle, he fought in files of six (which allowed time for reloading) and was protected from the cavalry charge by the pikemen. When caught in hand-to-hand fighting as the battle progressed, he used the musket as a club. The 'matchlock' musket, which had a range of no more than two hundred yards, was replaced later in the war by the 'flintlock musket', the firing device of which removed all problems associated with the match during rainy or windy conditions.

Even so, the poorly-trained musketeer continued to face serious problems in handling his musket and its accessories. The musket rest was cumbersome to use alongside all the other equipment and was therefore frequently cast aside, making it difficult to hold the weighty musket steady; the bullets would often be too large to fit into the barrel and therefore needed to be gnawed down to size; while the bandoliers, which contained the charges of powder, were vulnerable to flying sparks in the heat of the battle.

Loading the Musket

The action first involved holding the weapon upright with its butt-end on the floor - then:

*taking a powder cartridge (or bandolier) and pouring its contents down the barrel
*taking the scouring stick (which was clipped to the underside of the barrel) and ramming home the charge
*ramming in a wad of paper or grass to hold the bullet in place
*taking out a bullet from the bullet bag and putting it down the barrel
*ramming in another wad to keep the bullet in place
*priming the musket by pouring a little fine powder from the flask onto the priming pan
*taking the smouldering end of the match (a cord which was wound round a finger) and clipping onto the firing cock)
*placing the musket barrel on the lintock (or musket rest)
*firing when ordered to do so.

This complicated procedure was very difficult for raw recruits at the start of the war.

Above: A musketeer in the firing position with the barrel firmly supported by the lintock. Note the smouldering match, the bandoliers and the powder flask. An original painting by Shane Feeney.
Below: A musketeer in the process of loading the musket and using the scouring stick to ram home the charge and the bullet. Contemporary woodcut. (Author's collection collection)

Pikemen

In theory at least, the pikeman carried a sword and a pike made of ash, which was sixteen feet in length and headed by a narrow metal spike. He wore back-and-breast plates, a gorget (or steel collar), tassets (or thigh guards) and a pointed 'morion' helmet. In defence, the pikemen stood shoulder-to-shoulder, forming a 'hedgehog' of pikes with musketeers firing in between them as they resisted the cavalry charge. In attack, as they advanced against the opposing infantry, they lunged forward at the enemy as they came to 'push of pike'. Once hand-to-hand fighting commenced, the pikeman would often throw down his pike and rely on his sword - a weapon that had already no doubt been blunted by the chopping of wood for the camp fire.

A pikeman wearing full armour. An early seventeenth-century Dutch print. (Author's collection).

As war progressed, armies dispensed with much of the pikeman's armour (which weighed twenty-four pounds) to lighten his load on the march. The men themselves also had the annoying habit of cutting the pike staves shorter to make them more manageable during the battle - even though pikemen were allegedly selected for their strength. An officer wrote: 'Some that were not strong enough for his pike on a windy day would cut off a foot and some two of their pikes, which is a damned thing to be suffered'.

Cavalry

By the start of the war in 1642, most of the cavalry on view were the lightly-armoured 'harquebusiers'. These wore back-and-breast plates over a buff coat, gauntlets and a 'lobster-tail' helmet with face bars for protection against sword cuts. They also carried a brace of pistols and a sword in the saddle, plus a carbine (or short musket) with a flintlock firing action. A few also carried pole-axes for use against the heavily-armoured cuirassiers (see below) - although its has to be said that many cavalry troops in the first year or so of the war were seriously short of all this equipment. The cavalry, which charged in a disciplined and solid formation up to ten abreast and three or even six ranks deep, was used increasingly as a shock device at the start of the battle to drive off the opposing cavalry and then break up the infantry formation. Once the infantry was in disarray, the cavalry would move in among the hapless troops to cut them down with the sword.

In addition to the harquebusiers, there were a number of 'cuirassiers' in action during the first year or so of the war. One of the most famous regiments of these was that commanded by Sir Arthur Haselrig at the Battle of Lansdown. The cuirassiers wore three-quarter suits of heavy armour, which was cleverly riveted in sections to provide a degree of mobility. This gave Haselrig's regiment their famous nickname, for according to the Earl of Clarendon: 'they were so prodigiously armed that they were called by the other side the Regiment of Lobsters, because of the bright iron shells with which they were covered'. The men were armed with a sword and two pistols. This type of cavalry quickly became unfashionable, partly because it was extremely expensive to produce and partly because its sheer weight slowed down the horses at a time when the speed of the charge had become important.

Above: A harquebusier with light armour.
Below: A cuirassier with heavy suits of armour. Paintings by Shane Feeney.

Dragoons

The dragoon was a mounted infantryman who used his horse for mobility. Equipped with a flintlock musket or carbine, his task was to clear the flanks of the battlefield of enemy snipers, to provide cross-fire from hedgerows once the battle was joined, to act as a rear-guard or van-guard for an army on the march and to hold bridges or other strategic points. The dragoons rode ten abreast, but dismounted to fight with one of them detailed to look after the horses.

Artillery

A number of light field guns accompanied the marching armies to provide an artillery bombardment at the start of the battle aimed at breaking up the enemy formation. They were of little use once the battle had been joined. As they were extremely difficult to move in a

hurry, they were frequently captured by the enemy as soon as ground had been lost. They took four minutes to load and were guarded by 'fusiliers'. The guns most frequently used were the culverin (firing an 18-pound shot with a maximum range of 2,000 yards and requiring 8 horses to draw it); the demi-culverin (9-pound shot; range 1,800 yards; 7 horses); the saker (5-pound shot; range 1500 yards; 5 horses); and the falcon (2.5-pound shot; range 1200 yards; 2 horses).

Battle Formation and Tactics

On even ground in ideal circumstances, the army would draw up with regiments of infantry in the centre interspersed with a number of light field guns; cavalry regiments on the flanks with reserve regiments held behind in the centre; dragoons in hedges to guard the perimeter of the battlefield; heavy artillery on raised ground behind the army; and a 'forlorn hope' of muskets placed ahead of the front line under the cover of a ditch.

At the start of the battle, the sequence of action was as follows:
1. the dragoons would clear neighbouring hedges of enemy snipers;
2. artillery and musketeers would launch a bombardment to break up the enemy front line formation;
3. the forlorn hope muskets would fire in upon the ensuing confusion;
4. the cavalry would charge on both flanks, dispersing the enemy cavalry before turning in to attack the opposing infantry from flank and rear;
5. the infantry would then advance, coming to 'push of pike and butt end of musket'.

Battlefield Casualties

During the English Civil War, it is estimated that the 650 or so military engagements (battles, sieges and skirmishes) resulted in around 85,000 men killed in action and a similar number wounded. A further 117,000 soldiers were taken prisoner (including 83,000 royalists), while approximately 100,000 civilians and troops died of disease - particularly in towns and garrisons under siege. All-in-all about 12.3% of the adult male population in England died in the wars out of a total of around 1.5 million. It is also calculated that some 10% of adult males found themselves under arms at any one time at the peak of the war and that between 20% and 25% actually fought at some time for at least a short period.

Types of Injury

During a battle, horrific wounds could be inflicted by musket, sword, pike and cannon - especially when armies entered into hand-to-hand combat. Richard Wiseman, a surgeon with the royalist in the west from late 1643, describes in his diary what happened when the cavalry set about infantry soldiers at close quarters with their swords:

> They cruelly hack them; the poor soldiers sheltering their heads with their arms, sometimes the one, then the other, until they be both most cruelly mangled...And if the man flee, the enemy pursue; his hinder parts meet with great wounds, as over the thighs, back, shoulder and neck.

This description of the sufferings of the infantry is also confirmed by a parliamentarian source, John Vicars:

> They were most woefully cut and mangled, some having their ears cut off, some the flesh of their heads sheered off, some with their very skull hanging down and waiting to fall.

Even so, the pikemen often scored hits of their own against the cavalry. It is perhaps significant that many injuries sustained by horse riders were deep wounds to the thigh caused by the thrust of a pike.

However, by far the worst type of wound came as a result of either case-shot [a form of shrapnel fired by a cannon] or musket fire. Richard Wiseman, for instance, describes how one man sustained horrendous wounds from case-shot at the siege of Taunton:

> His face, with his eyes, nose, mouth and foremost part of the jaw, with the chin, was shot away and the remaining parts of then driven in. One part of the jaw hung down by his throat and the other part pushed into it. I saw the brain working out underneath the lacerated scalp on both sides between his ears and brows.

Wiseman did what he could to treat and feed the man by pouring milk down his throat - and he remained alive for several days afterwards.

Injuries from cannonballs could be equally devastating. The parliamentarian news-sheet, *A Perfect Diurnal*, describes, for instance, how royalist officer, Lord Moon, '*had his foot shot off with a cannon bullet*'. Injuries caused by musket fire were difficult to treat, especially where the flesh had been badly mangled by the entry of the bullet - or the bone seriously splintered resulting in many floating fragments within the wound. In cases such as these, the major risk was that of infection.

Three officers of the royalist army, which fought at Lansdown, each sustained bullet wounds at the ensuing siege of Bristol

When battle was joined, the infantry came to 'push of pike and butt end of musket'. Hand-to-hand fighting like this resulted in serious wounds to the face and head - see below.
(Line drawing by Stephen Beck).

- but with different outcomes. Gangrene quickly took hold of Nicholas Slanning's injury as it '*swelled, grew black and stank*'. He died later that night. Lord Grandison, however, lingered on for much longer, even though an infection had entered his leg wound. '*Although he was carried to Oxford and thought past danger,*' wrote a friend, '*he died two months later*'. On the other hand, Lord Belasyse, also wounded by musket fire at Bristol, survived for forty-three years with a piece of bullet lodged in his head.

Sir Edmund Ludlow recalls in his memoirs that, at the siege of Wardour Castle in 1644, one of his junior officers was extremely lucky to escape infection:

> *He was shot through the body and into the thigh by some of enemy from an ambuscade. Being brought to Southampton and his wound being searched, the bullet that went in at his belly was found at the chine of his back with a piece of waistband from his breeches - which, being cut out, he is wonderfully recovered.*

When the armies came to 'push of pike and butt end of musket', injuries were almost inevitable. Once battle was joined in this way, musketeers resorted to using their muskets as clubs. Holding the barrel (which was four feet in length), the musketeer could achieve considerable leverage, which could then be used to devastating effect - as Corporal Rowland Humfrey of Devizes found to his cost at the siege of Reading. There he sustained '*a great blow with a musket in the mouth, which beat out almost all his teeth besides the cutting of his lips*'.

Treatment of Injuries

Although medicine was still in its early stages, the London Company of Barber-Surgeons had already been established by the outbreak of the Civil War. A similar group had also been set up in Bristol at Barbers' Hall, which boasted a fine examination hall and dissecting room together with a large number of apothecaries, physicians and surgeons.

In the army, each regiment would include in its strength - at least in theory - one surgeon with two assistants, suitably equipped with a 'surgeon's chest' containing medical instruments, ointments, potions and powders. It was vital that wounds sustained in combat were treated initially on the battlefield - otherwise, as Richard Wiseman pointed out, infections quickly took hold. Wounds which were left several days before dressing, he said, were invariably 'full of maggots'. Similarly he believed that if limbs needed amputation, then it should be done immediately. 'Cut it off quickly...in the heat of the fight' while they are still in a daze over the incident - for then 'the limb is taken off much easier'.

Wherever possible at the end of the battle, army commanders would do their best to transport their wounded soldiers to a hospital in the nearest town under their control. According to eyewitnesses, in March 1643, after a bloody skirmish near Higham, near Gloucester, 'five wagons full of maimed soldiers were sent to Cirencester for relief', while a further 'eighteen wain loads of maimed men were brought to Oxford'. In September of that year, after the siege of Gloucester, Sir Samuel Luke's spy witnessed four hundred invalids being transported by boat to Bristol by river, plus a further three hundred sent 'to Cirencester and thereabouts in forty carts'.

Nevertheless, it was not always possible to deal with the wounded in this way, especially if the defeated army had been driven ruthlessly from the battlefield. In such instances, the wounded were invariably left to the mercy of local people. Some were accommodated in inns, while others were cared for by local householders and herbalists. The parish or town council often paid for the food and medicine required.

Treatment, whether at the hands of a regimental surgeon or a local one, was always a most unpleasant experience. A soldier, already experiencing intense pain from a musket bullet embedded in his thigh, for instance, was never offered herbs with sedative or pain-killing properties - partly, because surgeons feared accusations of witchcraft and partly, because they believed that pain actually assisted the healing process.

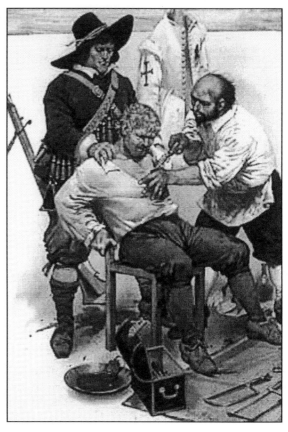

A surgeon removing a musket bullet. (An original painting by Angus McBride - courtesy of © Osprey Publishing Ltd.)

The unfortunate patient, therefore, was usually held down by the surgeon's mate, while the surgeon himself applied the relevant range of medical tools from his chest - the probe to locate the bullet; the speculum to open up the wound more widely; the duck bill to remove debris, which had accompanied the bullet into the flesh (e.g. fragments of clothing) and to take out the bullet itself; the cauterising iron to control the bleeding; the 'tents' of bandage, which were pushed into the wound to prevent premature healing; and the needles and waxed thread to close up the flesh. As he endured his agony, the soldier would doubtless avoid casting his eye at the other tools in the chest, which would be used if amputation of a limb was later deemed necessary - the incision knife, the cat lip (or dismembering knife to cut the flesh around the bone), the cerra (or bone saw) and the amputating chisel and mallet (for removing shattered fingers and toes).

Source: Rory McCreadie, The Barber-Surgeon's Mate of the 17th Century (1997)

Burying the Dead

During the Civil War, officers on the whole treated the dead of both sides with respect, regarding it as their Christian duty to provide as dignified a burial as conditions would allow. This often meant, at the end of the battle, that bodies would first be gathered up before being carried away in carts to be given mass burials in large pits dug nearby. If time permitted, the commanding officer would then arrange for prayers to be said, psalms sung, drums beaten and volleys of shot fired in a dignified ceremony to honour the dead

This of course was not usually possible, although commanders frequently showed courtesy by giving permission for the enemy to recover their dead from territory which had been captured from them. More often than not, however, bodies were hurriedly buried in shallow graves - as was true after the Battle of Naseby with the result that, according to one observer, 'the bodies in a short time became very offensive'. This sort of situation meant that people in local villages, fearful of the spread of disease, undertook the task of dealing with any unburied or poorly-buried bodies themselves.

The result of all this is that very few marked graves of civil war soldiers or monuments to their memory actually exist. One glorious exception is the fine effigy of Edward St John in the church of Lydiard Tregoz, near Swindon, killed in battle in 1645.

Women (known as 'camp followers') often accompanied the army and
performed useful tasks including cooking, washing, looking after
children and attending to the injured.
Line drawing by Stephen Beck.

7

The War Closes in on Bath, 1643

The King's Master Plan

The year 1642 had ended badly for the king. After raising his standard at Nottingham in August, he had been joined from the continent by his two nephews, Prince Rupert and Prince Maurice (both experienced soldiers). His attempts to regain London, however, had been thwarted first at the indecisive Battle of Edgehill in October and then by the reverse sustained at Turnham Green in November as his armies began their approach on the capital. By December, he had withdrawn to Oxford where he now set up his new headquarters. His hopes of a speedy victory had all but vanished for he was short of troops, short of cash and short of foreign support. Furthermore, the navy had defected to parliament, while most of the ports were now firmly under its control.

By February 1643, however, the king's prospects had brightened up considerably. The Earl of Newcastle had raised an army of 8,000 men for the royalist cause and was advancing towards York; a newly-recruited Cornish army under Sir Ralph Hopton and Sir Bevil Grenvile had defeated parliamentary forces at Braddock Down; and Queen Henrietta Maria had landed at Bridlington from her special mission to the continent, bringing back money and supplies. Encouraged by these developments, Charles now determined on a new major offensive to recapture London. His idea was to organise a coordinated thrust on the capital by his three field armies (i.e. Newcastle's, Hopton's and his own Oxford-based force).

1643: the king's plan for a coordinated attack on London.

The Advance of Hopton's Army

The Cornish army was brilliantly led by Hopton, a Somerset landowner from Witham Friary, who had finally persuaded the Cornishmen to do the unthinkable - namely to fight outside their native county. Winning skilful victories at Launceston in Cornwall and Stratton in Devon, he advanced northwards at the impressive rate of twenty miles a day, entering Somerset on 4 June. There, at Chard, he was joined by reinforcements sent by the king from Oxford under the Marquis of Hertford and Prince Maurice. Taunton quickly fell and by 12 June Hopton's victorious forces were already marching towards Wells.

Although Hopton was no doubt pleased to have bolstered his small army with the fresh troops from Oxford, he had mixed feelings about the arrival of Hertford and Maurice. Indeed, the king immediately appointed the marquis as nominal commander of the force by virtue of his courtly status - and the prince as lieutenant-general of horse. This was to prove a disastrous combination, as the Earl of Clarendon commented. Nobody at the time, he later wrote, believed that these appointments *would produce any good effect, there being no two men of more contrary natures and dispositions.*

On the one hand, the scholarly marquis was lazy by nature, *loving his ease and abhoring any fatigue, and having no military quality but courage in which he abounded.* Indecisive and self-

Sir Ralph Hopton (1596-1652). Portrait by an unknown artist. By courtesy of the National Portrait Gallery, London.

indulgent, he had little flair for leadership. On the other hand, the prince, who was the brother of Prince Rupert, was German by birth with few social graces; a rough, uncouth character whose manner was deeply offensive to refined courtiers. Nor were these weaknesses redeemed by any noticeable military flair. Indeed, according to Clarendon, *he understood very little more of the war than to fight very stoutly when there was occasion.* For his part Hopton, who was good at man-management and a decent tactician, took over the role of marshal of the field (and effective commander). His task, however, was not easy. The high command bristled with tension, uncertainty and indecision - weaknesses which badly undermined the effectiveness if the army (as will be demonstrated on several occasions during the ensuing campaign).

The Arrival of Waller's Army in Bath

Meanwhile, shocked by the ominous advance of the royalist army, parliament had taken swift action to preserve its grip on the west. Sir William Waller, whose first wife lay buried in Bath Abbey, was appointed major-general of all their western forces. His military exploits in the early months of the war in the south of England - with victories at Farnham Castle, Winchester and Chichester - had already earned him the nickname of 'William the Conqueror'. Reaching Bath on 15 March, he brought with him a professional expertise which few armies could boast at this stage of the war.

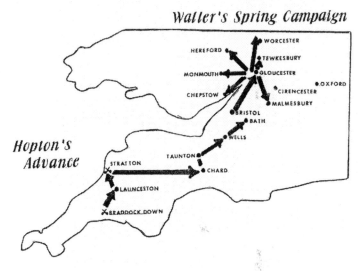

His first priority was to tighten his control of the Severn Valley, which lay to his rear, thus driving a vital wedge between the king in Oxford and his rich recruitment and supply grounds in Wales. Waller accomplished his objective in a lightening Spring campaign, which lasted a month. This saw the capture of Malmesbury, Tewkesbury, Chepstow and Cirencester, as well as the successful defence of both Bristol and Gloucester. By the end of April, Waller's rear had been secured as he faced up to the threat of Hopton's rapidly approaching army. However, a serious shortage of both infantry and cash threatened to undermine the strength of his position. He became caught up in endless squabbles with Colonel Nathaniel Fiennes, governor of the Bristol garrison (where Alexander Popham's Bath regiment was based) about the need to release more garrison troops to bolster his flimsy field army.

Hopton Reaches Bradford-on-Avon

Meanwhile the royalists had continued their relentless advance. Waller sent out a body of cavalry, dragoons and infantry under Popham to probe their position near Glastonbury. Although this force wisely decided against engagement (for it was heavily outnumbered), the royalists nevertheless gave merciless chase to Popham's men as they retreated in disarrary across the Mendips. The parliamentarians were badly mauled in a bloody skirmish after merciless attacks by cavalry under the command of Prince Maurice and the Earl of Carnarvon. Following this episode, both sides agreed on a temporary truce to enable them to lick their wounds and exchange prisoners - Waller gathering his forces around him in Bath and Hopton camping his army at Wells.

After the truce had ended, the royalists advanced to Frome. This move was the signal for an intensification of military activity as the two armies prepared themselves both mentally and physically for a major confrontation. According the the Earl of Clarendon, *no day now passed without action and regular sharp skirmishes*. The whole area became alive with cavalry patrols and keen-eyed scouts. Hearing from one such scout that two regiments of royalist cavalry had been billeted in the village of Stoke Lane, Waller sent Major Francis Dowett with a small cavalry force to discomfort them. Attacking at dawn, Dowett's men caught the royalists totally by surprise. Grenades were hurled into the cottages which were crowded with sleeping troops. In the ensuing confusion, over a hundred soldiers and one hundred-and-forty horses were captured along with a welcome haul of pistols. Not to be deterred by this setback, however, Hopton continued his advance, reaching Bradford-on-Avon on Sunday 2 July.

Sir William Waller (1579-1668). Portrait attributed to E. Bower.
(By courtesy of the National Portrait Gallery, London).

The Armies at Lansdown

The Royalists

Army: 6300 men (4000 infantry, 2000 cavalry, 300 dragoons, 16 field guns)

Leaders: The Marquis of Hertford (Nominal Commander)
Sir Ralph Hopton (Marshal of the Field)
Prince Maurice (Commander of Cavalry)

Regiments: According to Peter Young, there were in this Western Army:

Nine cavalry regiments under these colonels - Prince Maurice, the Earl of Carnarvon, Thomas Howard, Sir Humphrey Bennet, the Marquis of Hertford, Lord Hopton - plus the Marquis of Hertford's Lifeguard.

Nine infantry regiments under these colonels - Sir Bevil Grenvile, Sir Nicholas Slanning, John Trevanion, William Godolphin, Lord Mohun, Joseph Bamfield, the Marquis of Hertford, Prince Maurice and Brutus Bude.
The best of these were the five Cornish regiments of volunteers raised in 1642; three of the others had been recruited by Hertford on his march westwards to join Hopton; while another under Bamfield was weak and therefore confined to guarding the artillery train.
(Source: Peter Young: *The Praying Captain - A Cavalier's Memoirs*)

The Parliamentarians:

Army: 4600 men (1500 infantry, 2500 cavalry, 600 dragoons, ? field guns)

Leaders: Sir William Waller (Commander)
Sir Arthur Haselrig (Commander of Cavalry)
Colonel James Carr (General of Foot and Dragoons)

The actual *composition of the regiments* is less clear, but certainly included cavalry regiments commanded by Sir Arthur Haselrig, Sir William Waller and Colonel Robert Burghill; infantry regiments by Colonel Tom Essex, Colonel Tom Stephens and Sir Robert Cooke (many of these troops were drawn from Gloucestershire); and a dragoon regiment by Sir William Waller.

Friends Divided by War

Hopton and Waller

As the two army commanders waited during the temporary truce - Hopton in Wells and Waller in Bath - both men realised that in a matter of days they would be facing each other on the field of battle. The drama of the situation was heightened even further by the fact that they had been the closest of friends in their youth - a friendship strengthened by shared adventures on the continent in the Thirty Years' War. As young men, they had fought together as volunteers in the Elector of Palatine's army in 1620 - and, after the Battle of the White Mountain, they had jointly escorted the 'Winter Queen' (Charles I's sister, Elizabeth) on her retreat from Prague in 1621.

During the 1630s, both men had shared many of the religious beliefs of the leading puritan gentry. When parliament reassembled in 1640, both Hopton (as MP for Wells) and Waller (as MP for Andover) were highly critical of the king's policies and demanded the reform of abuses. Indeed, Hopton actually became a leading spokesman in 1641, presenting Charles with parliament's list of grievances in the Grand Remonstrance.

However, by 1642, Hopton had become one of the king's most outspoken supporters, even defending his attempt to arrest the Five Members (see page 4). A moderate reformer with little interest in party politics, he had become weary of extremists and fearful of rebellion. By July 1642, he had been expelled from parliament as a royalist. Waller, on the other hand, felt that the liberties of England were now at stake and were best defended by supporting the parliamentary cause.

Just before the two old friends met face-to-face on the battlefield at Lansdown, Waller - during that temporary truce - wrote a most moving and quite extraordinary letter to his old friend in which he deeply regretted 'the present distance' between them. Although he felt that (under God's guidance) they each had 'to be true to the cause' which they served, he detested 'this war without an enemy'. Drawn by fate into this terrible predicament, he concluded that they were 'both upon the stage and must act those parts' that had been assigned to them in this tragedy'.

WALLER'S LETTER TO HOPTON

To my noble friend, Sir Ralph Hopton at Wells.

Sir

The experience I have had of your worth and the happiness I have enjoyed in your friendship are wounding considerations when I look upon this present distance between us. Certainly my affection to you is so unchangeable that hostility itself cannot violate my friendship in your person. But I must be true to the cause wherein I serve...

...That great God, which is the searcher of my heart, knows with what a sad sense I go upon this service, and with what a perfect hatred I detest this war without an enemy; but I look upon it as the work of the Lord, which is enough to silence all passion in me. The God of peace in his good time send us peace, and in the meantime fit us to receive it. We are both upon the stage and must act those parts that are assigned to us in this tragedy. Let us do it in a way of honour and without personal animosities. Whatsoever the issue be, I shall never willingly relinquish the dear title of ...

Your affectionate friend and faithful servant

William Waller

Part of the actual letter. (By courtesy of Mr P.J.N. Prideaux-Brune of Prideaux Place, Nr Padstow)

The Lansdown Campaign: Phase I

Preliminary Manoeuvres: 3-4 July

Skirmish at Monkton Farleigh

With the royalists now in Bradford-on-Avon - a town no more than five miles from Bath - the stalemate had finally been broken. Although Hopton and Hertford initially had thoughts of pushing straight on to Oxford, Bristol was seen as too a rich prize as it dangled temptingly before their eyes. Indeed, the Earl of Essex (commander-in-chief of all parliament's armies) had already described that city as 'the key to the West of England', while both sides realised its value as a port, a lucrative source of customs duties and a centre for the manufacture of weapons of war - and Bath was the gateway to those riches. It was therefore decided to approach the city along the north side of the Avon river and to seek an early opportunity to encounter the enemy.

In the meantime, Waller had assembled the whole of his army on the flat top of Claverton Down with his guns on the ridge. This gave him a commanding view of the Avon valley beneath and the two roads which led from Bradford (one on each side of the river). Just below this strong position he had built a temporary bridge across the river right next to the ford near Claverton Manor (see map). Having secured this crossing by digging earthworks defences in Ham Meadow (an island in the middle

View of Waller's position on Claverton Down as gained by the royalist army across the Avon Valley as they advanced from Bradford-on-Avon.
(Author's collection)

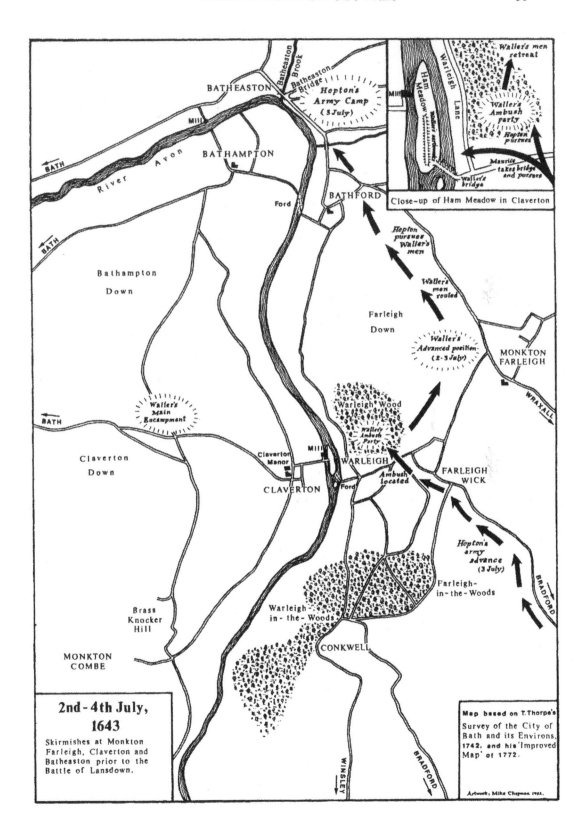

Close-up of Ham Meadow in Claverton

2nd - 4th July,
1643

Skirmishes at Monkton
Farleigh, Claverton and
Batheaston prior to the
Battle of Lansdown.

Map based on T. Thorpe's
Survey of the City of
Bath and its Environs,
1742, and his 'Improved
Map' of 1772.

Artwork: Mike Chapman 1992.

of the river), he then sent Colonel Burghill and Sergeant-Major Dowett with a detachment of some three hundred cavalry, dragoons and infantry under the cover of darkness over the river. These troops were then deployed at Monkton Farleigh on the high wooded slopes overlooking the route from Bradford with a small detachment detailed to set an ambush near the road itself.

Early on the following morning (3 July) the royalist cavalry advance guard encountered that ambush, but managed to hang on until the arrival of the rest of the army. A fierce struggle then ensued for one or two hours as the might of the Cornish infantry first drove the ambush party out of their lair and then - with support from the royalist cavalry - pushed up the hill to tackle the remainder of the enemy force at Monkton Farleigh. Heavily outnumbered, Burghill and Dowett wisely decided to retreat, scurrying away to the safety of Bath. They were, however, hotly pursued and harried by Hopton's cavalry through Bathford and as far as Batheaston. In the process of all this fighting, the parliamentarians lost two small field guns and suffered a number of casualties - although eyewitness accounts give conflicting estimates of the actual figures (see panel).

EVIDENCE FOR THE CASUALTIES AT THE AMBUSH

Contemporary accounts in wartime are inevitably biassed and are therefore to be treated with caution. It is, however, interesting to compare conflicting versions and to note how evidence is sometimes distorted or exaggerated.

Royalist version: (Colonel Slingsby)

We draw out presently and march towards the place [i.e. the ambush]...*from thence (though with a very hot dispute) they [the parliamentarians] were removed with the loss of two small pieces [i.e. cannons] and near one hundred men.*

Parliamentarian version: (John Vicars)

Major Dowett called off his men in the best order he could, which was so well performed that he lost only ten common soldiers and two hammer pieces through the gunners' negligence. We took of theirs thirteen prisoners, whereof one was a captain. Yet, for all this, the enemy boasted (as is their manner) of a great defeat [i.e. a defeat of Dowlett's force].

It was just as the royalists were pursuing the enemy in this chase that they first noticed Waller's main position on the top of Claverton Down and his bridge across the river. Prince Maurice immediately sent the main body of Cornish infantry down to the river to take the bridge and the earthworks in Ham Meadow, which Waller had lined with musketeers and dragoons. This was achieved by nightfall after fierce fighting and courageous defence. Seeing that the royalists now commanded the river crossing, Sir William Waller sensibly decided to withdraw his main force from Claverton Down into the safety of the walled city -

for he could not risk leaving either his army unprotected on the down or the city itself unguarded from within.

The Failed Attempt on Lansdown

Meanwhile the royalist army found itself widely dispersed with the Cornish infantry now on the Claverton side of the river,

The bridge built by Waller over the Avon below Claverton village, enabling him to move troops into their ambush position. Line drawing by Stephen Beck.

Hopton's cavalry (after the pursuit of Burghill's men) in fields beyond Batheaston and Hertford's remaining force struggling to rejoin the others. According to Slingsby, it had been their original intention 'to march directly up to Lansdown Hill' from which commanding position they could then launch an attack on Bath next day. However, in view of the dispersal of the troops, the onset of darkness and 'the narrow and craggy passage up the hill', it was decided at a midnight council of war to delay the advance and quarter the night instead in the meadows near Batheaston Bridge.

Just before daybreak, the royalist camp was astir. Men horses, cannon and baggage moved hastily away, according to Hopton, 'with a little more heat than was altogether expedient' towards the foothills of Lansdown. With some difficulty, the carriages and wagons were manoeuvred into a field on the lower slopes when, suddenly, the horrible truth dawned. Waller had beaten them to it! As the royalist commanders looked up to the high ridge above, they could see the parliamentarian army already assembled with their guns in position pointing ominously down the slope.

Waller was beginning to show his real craft and generalship, Always renowned for his rapid night marches (indeed, his other nickname was 'The Night Owl'), his ascent of Lansdown in the early hours of the morning had dramatically snatched the initiative out of the royalists' hands. Furthermore, Hertford had now placed his army in an unenviable position. The heavy guns and baggage carts were almost inextricably wedged in the small, muddy fields at the bottom of Lansdown, 'out of which', as Hopton wrote, 'there were very inconvenient ways to retreat, to advance no possibility and to stay there least of all, for the enemy's

Waller's position on the southern ridge of Lansdown, which gave him a commanding view of the royalist army below in the fields on the lower slopes. Author's collection.

cannon played into them'.

Withdrawal to Marshfield

For several hours the armies faced each other. According to Slingsby, 'we spent that day looking upon each one another', the enemy getting a really good view of the size of the royalist army, which was far too large 'to tempt him down to fight'. Five parliamentarian guns continued to blaze down on the royalist position as the commanders debated their next move. About one in the afternoon - after considerable dithering - they eventually decided to withdraw their forces to Marshfield, a village four miles north of their present position and six miles north-east of Bath. From there, they argued, it would be possible either to approach Lansdown from the northern end or to continue their journey to Oxford. Hopton was given the task of ordering the army's retreat.

It turned out to be a tricky and difficult operation. Two narrow lanes with high flanking hedges led to Marshfield (much as they do today), winding their way upwards to the ridge on which the village stood. The cannon and baggage train, sent first under escort, struggled furiously to get clear. Meanwhile, Hopton had

Royalist supply wagons stuck in the mud on the lower slopes of Lansdown. Line drawing by Stephen Beck.

planted one thousand musketeers in the hedges at the entrance to these lanes to give cover to the rest of the army as it retreated. He personally remained behind with a strong cavalry rearguard to hold off sniping attacks from Waller's horse and dragoons. The withdrawal was successfully completed with considerable flair and skill. Billets were found for many troops that night in Marshfield, Cold Ashton and nearby villages, while others camped in the fields outside.

CONFLICTING EVIDENCE: RETREAT TO MARSHFIELD

Hopton's Account:

Sir Ralph Hopton then sent off the [royalist] army in parts, remaining only to hold up the enemy with a strong forlorn hope of horse, with which at last he marched off without any loss. He drew a strong party of the enemy's horse within the ambusade of musketeers [i.e. those which lined the hedges along the lanes], which having tasted they quickly retired. And so the army came that night safe to Marshfield.

Vicar's Account:

Hopton's cavalry rearguard, when pressed by Waller's cavalry, he said, retreated speedily...

...without striking one stroke; and left behind them three hundred weight of bullets... Our party chased them to Marshfield, and that night gave them a sound alarm, but not one of them stirred, although they had bragged to be in Bath that night; for they wisely decided that, after so hot a chase, the water in Bath would have been too hot for them, which might have produced a fatal malignant fever upon them.

Royalist musketeers line the hedges along the lanes leading to Marshfield to provide cover for the rest of the army. Line drawing by Stephen Beck.

9

The Lansdown Campaign:
Phase II

Approach to Battle: 5 July - morning

The battle, which is described over the following pages, was fought on and around Lansdown, a plateau some two miles in length. Situated to the north-west of Bath, it rises steeply on all sides and is bounded by sharp ridges. Hedges, walls, narrow tracks and wooded slopes dominated the surrounding landscape at the time. The very nature of the terrain therefore ensured that normal civil war battle formations and tactics (as described in Chapter 6) could not be used on this occasion. In consequence, much of the preliminary fighting consisted of skirmishing and manoeuvering for position.

Skirmishes on Tog Hill

Early on the morning of Wednesday 5 July Sir William Waller again anticipated the royalists' next move by advancing his parliamentarian forces along the flat top of Lansdown and establishing a new position on the far northern escarpment overlooking the road from Marshfield. There on the very edge of the down (with a valley some 225 feet below) he rapidly constructed a long line of breastworks, constructed out of earth, timber and stone - defences which stretched right across both the road and the various tracks leading up the steep slope. From here Waller sent out parties of horse to reconnoitre the enemy's position. These successfully located and attacked the royalists' cavalry pickets outside Marshfield, forcing them to sound the alarm.

Shortly afterwards, at about 8 o'clock, the royalist army left its Marshfield encampment and marched in the direction of Lansdown along (in the words of one observer) 'a continuing plain large field', which ran from Marshfield to Tog Hill (a distance of some three miles). As it drew nearer, the officers suddenly noticed - much to their dismay - the enormous strength of the parliamentarian position. Colonel Slingsby, a royalist commander who had already praised Waller as 'the best shifter and choser of ground', described their initial impression:

We could see the rebels' army drawn up upon the top of the hill, he upon a piece of ground almost inaccessible. In the brow of the hill he had raised breastworks in which his cannon and great store of small shot was placed; on either flank he was strengthened with a thick wood which stood upon the declining of the hill, in which he had put store of musketeers; on his rear he had a fair plain where stood ranged his reserves of horse and foot...Thus fortified stood the fox gazing at us.

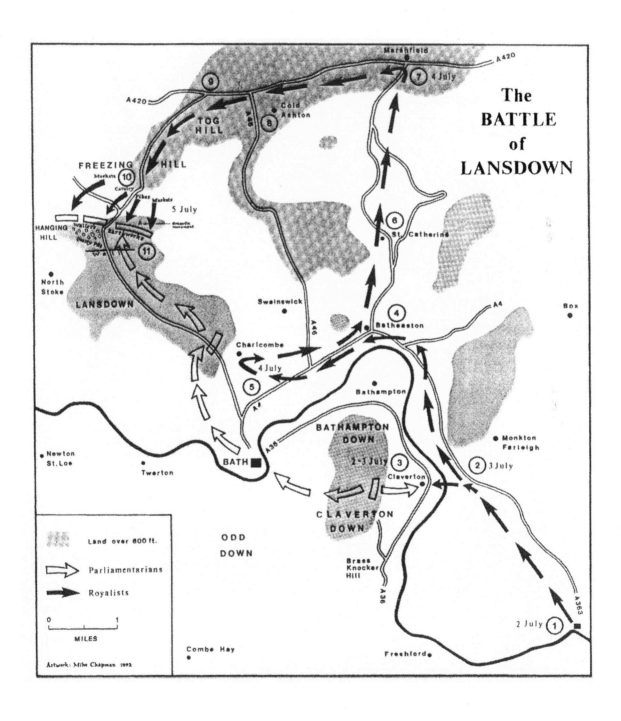

The
BATTLE
of
LANSDOWN

The royalist army's view from the cornfield on Tog Hill of Waller's position on the Lansdown ridge over a mile away. Author's collection

The royalists had halted in a large corn field on Tog Hill where they drew up in order of battle, hoping to engage the enemy there and then. As the two armies gazed at each other through the morning mist, they were separated by a steep valley and a mile and a half in distance. A narrow lane with high hedges ran from the cornfield (much as it does today) down Tog Hill and Freezing Hill before plunging steeply into the bottom and then rising sharply up onto the northern ridge of Lansdown.

For something like three or four hours little happened apart from light skirmishing by dragoons in the hedges around the cornfield and small parties of horse on the flanks. Eventually the royalist commanders decided that Waller was unlikely to be drawn down from his favourable position and that this sort of haphazard skirmishing was merely wasting their ammunition, of which there was already a shortage. The order was therefore given to withdraw in an orderly fashion back to Marshfield.

They had scarcely retreated a mile when they looked round to see a large body of Waller's cavalry and dragoons led by Colonel Carr and Major Dowett charging down the hill in their direction. Waller was clearly anxious to halt any possible advance on Oxford, which would enable Hopton to join forces with the king for an attack on London. The parliamentarian horse vigorously attacked the rear and flanks of the royalist army,

Dragoons skirmish around the hedges of the cornfield on Tog Hill. Line drawing by Stephen Beck

which was in marching column, routing two bodies of their cavalry. Eventually the Earl of Carnarvon's horse and Sir Nicholas Slanning's musketeers managed to salvage the situation.

Under this pressure, the royalist forces turned about yet again, hurrying to regain their former position in the cornfield which, according to Slingsby, they 'got with much difficulty and hazard'. Waller's cavalry was eventually driven out of the cornfield by a series of well-aimed valleys of musket fire. Their dragoons, too, were finally dislodged from the walls and hedges at the far end of the field by a determined advance of the Cornish foot. The roundhead horse now found itself trapped in the confines of the narrow lane which led to Lansdown.

Sensing his opportunity, Prince Maurice sent his own cavalry to 'wing' them by firing in through the hedges on both sides of the lane. Waller's men soon found themselves

The monument to Sir Bevil Grenvile on the battlefield site. This drawing by S.H. Grimm in 1789 shows the view from Waller's earthworks, uncluttered by present-day trees, of the royalist advance from Tog Hill (rear) and Freezing Hill (left). By permission of the British Library.

in a state of confusion and panic. Some fled 'in great disorder'. The situation, however, was partly retrieved when Waller sent down a second wave of more seasoned reinforcements - nine hundred cavalry and dragoons under Colonel Burghill. Richard Atkyns (captain of a royalist cavalry troop) admitted that 'this was the boldest thing that I ever saw the enemy do; for a party of less than 1,000 to charge an army of 6,000 horse, foot and cannon in their own ground, at least a mile and a half from their [main] body'.

Royalist Advance on Freezing Hill

The parliamentarians fought bravely for two or three hours before tiredness gradually overtook the foot soldiers, who had been sent into action to strengthen resistance. Although Waller tried hard to relieve these by sending down his reserve infantry, they proved too inexperienced to make good their ground. The rawness and inadequacy of his foot was already beginning to hamper the effectiveness of Waller's schemes on the battlefield. Finally, after stiff and prolonged fighting, a combined push by the Cornish foot and Carnarvon's horse drove the parliamentarians down Tog Hill and Freezing Hill. There, according to

Prince Maurice (1620-1652), brother of Prince Rupert and commander of the royalist cavalry at Lansdown. By courtesy of the Ashmolean Museum, University of Oxford.

Slingsby, they were routed in the bottom of the valley below and 'cruelly galled' by the royalist infantry. Waller's men scurried back up the slopes as best they could to the safety of the earthworks and the protection of the parliamentarian main force, which was still intact on the downs.

In spite of their casualties and the tiredness brought about by such a gruelling encounter, the royalists suddenly found a new determination. Colonel Slingsby made the point that the Cornish infantry were now so confident that they believed 'no men their equals and were so apt to undertake anything' - so much so, in fact, that even the enemy's seemingly impenetrable position on the top of the hill with cannon already blazing down on them 'could not deter them'.

According to royalist Richard Atkyns, this overconfidence had been deliberately encouraged by the parliamentarians in an attempt to draw the royalists into the death trap of the steep slopes. Waller, it appeared, had played the oldest trick in the military handbook - namely that of the feigned flight. Turning the rout of his skirmishing troops on Freezing Hill to his own advantage, he now gave the pretence that his whole army was in a state of total disorder. He therefore caused (Atkyns noted) 'the blowing up of powder; horse and foot running distractedly upon the edge of the hill' to give the impression that his forces were on the point of hasty retreat. Taken in by these signs of panic, Sir Robert Welsh begged Prince Maurice for permission 'to follow the chase' up the hill with a body of horse. The ploy had worked. Even the rugged Cornish infantry were now thoroughly roused. 'Let us fetch those cannon', they cried out to a man, irritated by the constant bombardment from above. It was a murderous decision, which brought into serious question the leadership of the royalist high command. Death could be the only victor in the inevitable bloodbath that followed.

The royalist Earl of Clarendon was later most scathing in his criticism of this decision, which was prompted as much as anything by a rush of blood to the Cornishmen's head. The royalist army, he suggested, should have waited patiently and 'neglected the enemy' until Waller's army was tempted down from its advantageous position. 'But the unreasonable contempt they had of the enemy and their confidence they themselves should prevail in *any* ground' (added to their shortage of provisions and 'their waste of ammunition...in the daily hedge skirmishes') undermined any hope of a patient approach. 'They therefore suffered themselves to be engaged upon a great disadvantage'.

The Earl of Carnarvon (right), who commanded a royalist cavalry regiment at Lansdown. Section of a print entitled 'Charles I Surrounded by his Supporters'. By courtesy of the Ashmolean Museum, University of Oxford.

Enemy Praise for Waller's Generalship

COLONEL SLINGSBY greatly admired Waller's ability to think one step ahead of his enemy by manoeuvring his forces into advantageous positions. He also praised the crafty manner in which Waller, 'the fox', forced the enemy to exhaust itself by dealing with ambushes and skirmishes, while he kept his own main force secure on impregnable ground. Furthermore, Waller - who was desperately short of infantry - managed to avoid any major engagement with the enemy except on terrain of his own chosing, where his strong cavalry could reign supreme. Slingsby's comments on all this are as follows:

The successful skirmish at Monkton Farleigh (3 July):

... we possessing this ground discovered the body of the enemy drawn up in battalia on the other side of the river...Thus had the shifting rebel deluded us one day with a [ambush] party, hoping to make us weary with dancing about him, or else to fight where he pleased.

Waller's position on the southern ridge of Lansdown (4 July)

[They found that Waller was already in possession of the hill] for with judgment observed our motion and discerned our intention - so that with great industry and care laboured all night to prevent us and secure himself of such an advantage. Indeed, that general of the rebels was the best shifter and choser of ground, when he was not the master of the field, that ever I saw; which are great qualities in a soldier.

Waller's position on the northern ridge of Lansdown (5 July)

We could see the rebels' army drawn up upon the top of the hill, he upon a piece of ground almost inaccessible...Thus fortified stood the fox gazing at us.

10

The Lansdown Campaign: Phase III

The Battle - Part One: 5 July afternoon

Royalist Advance on Lansdown

The whole royalist army, which had regrouped on Freezing Hill, now advanced to the foot of Lansdown. It was now about 5 o'clock in the afternoon. The royalist news-sheet, *Mercurius Aulicus*, vividly describes the challenge of the task facing them:

> *For the ground the enemy had was of mighty advantage, being a hill walled about behind and upon both sides, with [breast]works in front, the passage up very narrow and dangerous, one side being a wood, the other full of hedges, both strongly lined with musketeers.*

Hopton therefore sent strong parties of musketeers into the woods and hedges on each flank to clear out the enemy dragoons and then to work their way gradually to the top of the hill. Even the parliamentarian mayor of Bristol, who had received an eyewitness account from a released prisoner, praised the skill of these 'Cornish excellent firemen at their hedge fight in a little wood there adjacent' (although it was later commented by others that, in the process, 'much powder was spent' - wastage that the army could ill afford).

Meanwhile, Sir Bevil Grenvile led forward his regiment of Cornish foot with pikes astride the road in the centre and

The Cornish infantry begin their assault on the parliamentarian position. Line drawing by Stephen Beck

muskets on the left to seek cover behind the walls and hedges of various small enclosures. They were flanked on the right by the cavalry, which endeavoured to make the most of the slightly more open ground which, according to Slingsby, was 'best for horse'. Bravely they pushed forward in the face of an almighty pounding from Waller's muskets in the earthworks above.

Capture of the Earthworks

Slowly and courageously they inched their way up that impossible slope until finally their infantry gained a foothold in the earthworks, forcing the enemy to pull back its own infantry and artillery. It was at that point, however - according to

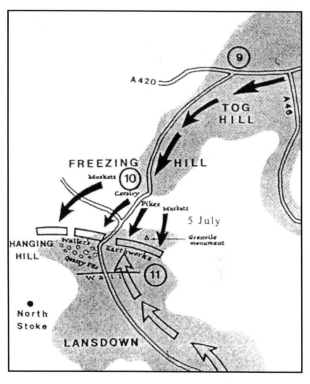

The final stages of the battle. Artwork by Mike Chapman.

parliamentarian Edward Harley - that Waller's 'whole body of horse charged them', not once but five times. The royalist news-sheet agreed:

The Cornish infantry storm the parliamentarian earthworks. Line drawing by Stephen Beck.

Having gotten his ground...before our horse and foot could draw up in battalia, they charged us with their horse, and played so thick upon us with their cannon and muskets, that they forced us from the hill - which, not withstanding, we assaulted again and again three several times; and the fourth time, with unimaginable difficulty, we possessed the top of it, which Sir Bevil Grenvile maintained with his stand of Cornish pikes against all their power of horse, foot and cannon, to the wonder and amazement of both friends and enemies.

Sir Arthur Haselrig. Portrait by Van Dyke.
Collection unknown; photograph © National
Portrait Gallery, London.

Although the royalist infantry had with considerable bravery managed to capture the earthworks, Waller's counter-attack had been so effective that 1400 out of the 2000 royalist cavalry present had fled the battlefield at speed, heading for Oxford where (according to Clarendon) they reported 'all to be lost'. The Cornish infantry who (in the words of several observers) had now been 'left naked', never forgave the cavalry for this shameful defection - referring to them henceforward in contemptuous terms as 'the runaway horse'.

The Earl of Clarendon, however, had an interesting explanation for this apparent cowardice. The fact of the matter was, he said, that the royalist cavalry had been terror-struck by the amazing sight of Haselrig's regiment of heavily-armoured cuirassiers ('The Lobsters') charging down on them. This was the first time that they had been seen by either side on the field of battle. Their sudden appearance therefore 'gave so great a terror to the king's horse, who had never before turned from an enemy' that they were unable to counter-charge. Indeed they were so terrified, he said, that the Lobsters 'totally routed them'. Part of the problem was that Haselrig's men were 'so prodigiously armed' and heavy [i.e. with three-quarter suits of armour] that the lightly-armoured royalist cavalry were not able to bear the 'shock' of the charge - besides which, with apparently impenetrable armour, 'they were secure from hurts of the sword'.

In the fury of the battle, Sir Bevil Grenvile himself was mortally wounded during one of those cavalry charges just as he reached the brow of the hill (see Chapter 11), while Sir Nicholas Slanning's horse was killed under him after being struck by a cannon ball. Having at last driven the enemy from their original position, the royalists now drew up their infantry and remaining cavalry into a new line on the top of the hill, taking cover in Waller's abandoned breastworks. Slingsby described with great satisfaction what he now saw: 'our foot leaps into their breastworks; our horse draws upon their ground; our two wings that were sent to fall into the two woods had done their business and were upon the hill as soon as the rest'.

Atkyns, however, was not entirely comfortable with the royalists' new position, which was 'upon the edge of a hill so steep that they could hardly draw up'. It was true, he agreed, that some additional cover was provided by 'shelves near the place like Romanish works, but so shallow that my horse had a bullet in his neck'. [These were in fact the ruined remains of a Roman pewter workshop - the grass-covered outline of which is still visible].

The Parliamentarian Withdrawal

Parliamentarian accounts of the struggle for the ridge admitted that the enemy had partly taken it by force, but also claimed that Waller had largely surrendered it by choice in a tactical decision. This was a wise judgment, according to the parliamentarian news-sheet, *A True Relation*: 'Considering our horse exceeded theirs in number as their foot did ours, we might now have sufficient room to fight with our horse'. Indeed, the flat top of Lansdown was much more suited to the cavalry charge than the steep wooded slopes beyond. Once the bulk of the royalist cavalry had fled, Waller was quite content to draw their weary, boodstained foot onto the top of the hill.

    Furthermore, it had clearly been an orderly and planned withdrawal - albeit under considerable pressure - for the parliamentarians had managed to tow away their valuable artillery to the safety of their new position. This was no mean task considering the number of horse required to do so. In most Civil War battles, the cannon was invariably lost to the enemy whenever a position was overrun. But whatever the truth of the matter, both royalist and roundhead agreed that it had been 'a very bloody and terrible fight'.

The northern ridge of Lansdown viewed from the spot where Cornish infantry stood their ground 'as immovable as a rock'. The monument was erected on the spot where Grenvile fell. Author's collection.

Eyewitnesses Describe the Heat of the Battle

Captain Richard Atkyns describes his own experiences during the assault:

As I went up the hill, which was very steep and hollow, I met several dead and wounded officers brought off; besides several running away, that I had much ado to get up by them. When I came to the top of the hill, I saw Sir Bevil Grenvile's stand of pikes, which certainly preserved our army from a total rout, with the loss of his most precious life. They stood as upon the eaves of a house for steepness, but as unmovable as a rock. On which side of this stand of pikes our horse were, I could not discover; for the air was so darkened by the smoke of the powder, that for a quarter of an hour together (I dare say) there was no light to be seen, but what the fire of the volleys of shot gave. And 'twas the greatest storm that ever I saw, in which I knew not whither to go nor what to do. My horse had two or three bullets in him presently, which made him tremble under me at that rate, that I could hardly with spurs keep him from lying down; but he did me the service to carry me to a led horse, and then died.

John Vicars, parliamentarian pamphleteer, admires the bravery of Sir Arthur Haselrig and others:

He and his London lads fought like so many invincible Romans...as long as light would suffer them to distinguish friends from foes. And we must do our enemies right, who fought it out very stoutly too; and indeed the charges were so incessantly hot on both sides, as the like (I believe) was never seen in England, no not at Kineton battle, yea some old soldiers did say.
[Kineton was the village nearest to the Battle of Edgehill in 1642]

Mercuricus Aulicus, royalist news-sheet (8 July 1643) pays tribute to one brave gentleman volunteer:

Master Leak, son of the Lord Daincourt, who with one troop charged three of the rebels' troops, where the brave gentleman was slain with four of the enemy dead on the ground and a colour taken of the rebels folded in his arms...He had a brother in the same troop (Master Charles Leak), who bravely revenged his brother's death.

Captain Edward Harley, parliamentarian cavalry officer, describes the charge:

The enemy pursued hotly and got that ground where our ordnance was planted, but then our whole body of horse charged with as much resolution as could be...Our regiment charged twice and, in the second, my bay horse was killed under me, but I thank God brought me off well in this hot service.

The heat of the battle on the Lansdown slopes. A line drawing by Stephen Beck.

11

Death of Sir Bevil Grenvile

Sir Ralph Hopton describes the moment when Sir Bevil was mortally wounded:

*Sir Bevil Grenvile then stood at the head of his regiment upon Tog Hill. Then Sir
Bevil advanced with a party of horse on his right hand (that ground being best
for them) and his musketeers on the left; himself leading up his pikes in the
middle. And, in the face of their cannon and small shot from their breastworks,
gained the brow of the hill having sustained two full charges of the enemy's
horse; but in their third charge, his horse falling and giving ground, he received,
after other wounds, a blow on the head with a pole-axe, with which he fell.*

Sir Bevil Grenvile is mortally wounded. Line drawing by Stephen Beck.

Sir Bevil's bodyguard, who was near to him when he fell, was Anthony Payne.
Known as 'The Cornish Giant' (for he allegedly stood seven feet and four inches
in height), he immediately lifted Sir Bevil's thirteen-year old son, John (often
called Jack), into his father's saddle so that a Grenvile would remain at the head of
the regiment.

 After the battle was over, Sir Bevil was carried under the cover of darkness
to the Rectory at Cold Ashton, which had been his billet on the previous night. It
was there in the dining room of that house that he died next day. The chair in
which he was sitting at the time was always pointed out to visitors for many

generations thereafter (though it no longer exists). Anthony Payne immediately set about writing the following sorrowful letter, which was despatched to Sir Bevil's wife, Grace, at Stowe (their home near Kilkhampton in Cornwall):

The Rectory at Cold Ashton, where Sir Bevil died on the day after the battle. Author's collection.

Honoured madam, ill news flieth apace. The heavy tidings no doubt have already travelled to Stowe that we have lost our blessed master by the enemy's advantage. You must not, dear lady, grieve too much for your noble spouse. You know, as we all believe, that his soul was in heaven before his bones were cold.

He fell, as he did often tell us he wished to die, in the great Stuart cause for his country and his king. He delivered to me his last commands and with such tender words for you and for his children as are not to be set down with my poor pen, but must come to your ears upon my heart's best breath.

Master John, when I mounted him upon his father's horse, rode him into the war like a young prince as he is; and our men followed him with their swords drawn and with tears in their eyes. They did say they would kill a rebel for every hair of Sir Bevil's beard. But I bade them remember their good master's word when he wiped his sword after Stamford's fight [i.e. the royalist victory at Stratton in May over the Earl of Stamford's parliamentarians]; *how he said, when their cry was 'stab and slay', 'Halt men, God will avenge'.*

I am coming with the mournfullest load that ever a poor servant did bear to bring their great heart that is cold to Kilkhampton vault [i.e. the family vault]. *O! my lady, how shall I ever brook your weeping face? But I will be truthful to the living and the dead.*

These, honoured madam, from thy saddest and truest servant, Anthony Payne.

Sir Bevil Grenvile (1596-1643). By courtesy of Ashmolean Museum, University of Oxford.

His body was carried back to Launceston and then on to Kilkhampton, where it was buried in the family vault. On his body was found a personal letter from the king, written on white silk. Grenvile, anticipating his possible death on the battlefield, had endorsed it with an instruction: 'Keep this safe'.

12

The Lansdown Campaign: Phase III

The Battle - Part Two: 5 July evening

Waller's New Position

Waller had now withdrawn to a new position about four hundred yards from his old earthworks behind a long stone wall, which ran across the down and a large adjoining sheepfold. There he re-formed his whole army, lining the wall with musketeers. In several places he broke down the stones to create large openings in the wall through which his cavalry could charge. These breaches were carefully guarded by his cannon and bodies of pikemen. Royalist Richard Atkyns was full of admiration for Waller's new position, which he declared was 'as good as defence against anything but cannon as could be'.

Both sides were by now in an exhausted state and were happy to take a breather. Indeed, according to the royalist news-sheet, *Mercuricus Aulicus*, the battle proper, which had started on Tog Hill and finished on Lansdown, 'lasted from two in the afternoon till one the next morning'. Clarendon agreed: 'each party was sufficiently *tired and battered* to be contented to stand still'. Slingsby, with his usual dry sense of humour, also took up a similar theme: 'Thus stood the two armies *taking breath* looking upon each other, our cannon on both sides playing without ceasing till it was dark - legs and arms flying apace'. Hopton, too, seemed to hint that the armies had really fought themselves to a standstill for 'each side played upon the other with their ordnance, but neither advanced *being soundly*

The wall behind which Waller's army withdrew. The monument can be seen in the distance. Author's collection.

battered'.

As dusk fell the repeated explosions of cannon fire could - according to the city's mayor - be both heard and seen in Bristol. It was during this bombardment that Hopton made another move. Although the two armies were well within the range of the light field guns, they were not within effective range of musket fire [i.e. a maximum of two hundred yards, whereas 'the wall' was four hundred yards away]. Hopton therefore - according to his own journal - moved his musketeers on the right wing to a more forward position 'much nearer their army' by 'lodging themselves amongst the many little pits betwixt the wall and the wood - from whence we galled them cruelly'. These old Anglo-Saxon quarry pits, which can still be seen today, provided ideal cover within musket range of the wall.

(Above) One of the repairs made to the wall later by local farmers (note the different stones used) to fill in the breaches created by Waller. (Both photographs from the author's collection) (Below) The quarry pits, which provided a forward position for royalist musketeers to fire at Waller's men behind the wall.

The Night-Time Volley

Guns were still blazing away when darkness finally parted the two armies - a fact which, according to parliamentarian John Vicars, 'hindered our total completing of victory'. After nightfall, there was an ominous silence for one or two hours. Then, at about one o'clock in the morning, the royalist army was suddenly startled by one great volley of musket fire coming from the parliamentarian lines - but then total silence. The royalists were mystified. According to Slingsby, 'some of us judged that he was retreating' and that this was his parting shot; but 'the general apprehension through our army was that the enemy had intention to try to push in the night for their ground' [i.e. to launch a sudden night attack]. By now, of course, they had become all too familiar with the sudden switches of position and night marches of Waller, 'the Night Owl'.

Nor is there any doubt that the royalists were in a nervous and edgy state. Slingsby admitted that the army was 'then seated like a heavy stone on the very brow of the hill, which with one lusty charge might well have been rolled to the bottom'. Many of the men had by now lost the will to fight. Indeed, according to royalist Richard Atkyns, their commanders had already given instructions that if the enemy fell upon them during the night, every man was 'to shift for himself'. Indeed, the cannon had already been moved off the hill to clear the way for any panic rush by the troops! A number of factors had shattered their morale - namely, the death of their beloved Grenvile; an acute shortage of ammunition; and the cowardice of the cavalry. As Slingsby pointed out: 'had our horse been as good as the enemy's, the rebels [would] never have gone off the field unruined'.

Meanwhile, the royalist high command scarcely knew what to do amid that eery silence. In the darkness it was extremely difficult to pick out anything in the roundhead camp apart from the glow of matches slung over the wall by the musketeers and stands of pikes silhouetted against the sky. For an hour, the commanders debated the situation. Eventually - according to Hopton - they decided to give 'a common soldier a reward to creep softly towards the place where the enemy stood'. After a long delay, he returned with the sensational news that Waller - the Night Owl - had vanished into the night with the whole of his army, leaving behind the glowing matches and stands of pikes as decoys to suggest that the army was still in camp. It has to be said that the royalists apparently breathed a collective sigh of relief. 'We were glad they were gone', commented Slingsby with his wry humour, 'for if they had not, I know who would have done so within the hour!'

Waller's Withdrawal to Bath

Waller had decided on a tactical withdrawal to Bath so that his men and horses could be refreshed. The parliamentarian news-sheet, *A True Relation*, explained that the major factor in the decision was '...our horse being in continual service for three days together, and without meat or water for the space of at least twenty-four hours, and our foot much tired'. Waller therefore had wisely used the resources available to him in the city (as he had done on the Monday night), again demonstrating his skill as a clever 'chooser and shifter of ground'. He also hoped to bolster up the numbers of his infantry by some overnight recruiting from both the local countryside and the Bristol garrison.

But Waller had of course no intention of staying in Bath. He fully realised that the royalists, with heavy casualties sustained by the infantry and large desertions by the cavalry, were now in no position to besiege Bath. Furthermore, he knew only too well (as John Vicars explained) that he 'could easily recover the hill again, and so fall upon the enemy to prosecute the victory next morning. Our retreat was so orderly and fairly performed, that the enemy durst not follow us, as having learned by experience that our giving ground hath been much to their disadvantage'.

WALLER'S LETTER TO THE SPEAKER

A week after the battle (once he had reached Devizes in pursuit of Hopton's army), Waller snatched a few minutes to scribble a few lines to the Speaker of the House of Commons giving a brief description of the battle at Lansdown.

Sir William Waller and Sir Arthur Haselrig the the Speaker Roundway this 12 July 1643

We cannot but give you a short account of some last passages amongst us through this last fortnight. We have had scarce leisure to eat or sleep and never more troubled that upon this time upon Wednesday was seven night [or 'sennight' - a week ago]. *We had a weary and dangerous day's fight, the night parting us and so well did we knock each other that in the night we both retreated. Many of their chief commanders and officers were slain or hurt. We lost only one sergeant-major of dragoons and two cornets and not twenty common soldiers.*

We had the advantage of the ground, but the Cornish hedgers [drove] us from it, though they bought it at a dear rate. When our foot left it, we maintained it with our horse, and those Sir Arthur Haselrig brought from London did excellent service...

We have had such experience of God that we doubt not to give you a good account of Sir Ralph Hopton. For the present he is miserably burnt with powder [see Chapter 14]...

THE PROBLEM OF DESERTION

Many of the troops who fought in the battle were raw, inexperienced volunteers or conscripts. They lacked the sort of discipline that was imposed later in the war by the New Model Army. It is hardly surprising, therefore, that many of them were traumatised by the horror of close-quarter fighting or that some eventually fled the battlefield in sheer terror. Desertions were by no means just limited to one side in the conflict.

A Perfect Diurnal (parliamentarian news-sheet)

About five hundred of the [royalist] *soldiers ran away, many of them being taken up by the country people and brought to Sir William. These took an oath never more to take up arms against the parliament and were let to return to their dwellings.*

John Vicars (parliamentarian)

Parliamentarian desertions: *At least 500 of our common soldiers who causelessly ran away.*

Richard Atkyns (royalist)

After listing those royalists who had been killed, injured or taken prisoner, he added: *and more than all these ran away to Oxford to carry the tidings of our defeat before it was!*

The Mayor of Bristol (parliamentarian)

Master John Ashe had his ground well stocked with sixty cavalier horses, who fled from the army the night after the battle.

The arrest of a deserter.
Line drawing by Stephen Beck

13

Who Had Actually Won?

Both sides claimed victory at the end of what had been a most exhausting and prolonged battle.

Parliamentarian Claims

The late success of the truly valiant and magnanimous commander, Sir William Waller, in the western parts and the victory obtained by him...on Wednesday July 5th near Marshfield...is already made public by many pens.
(Special Passages, 12-19 July, 1643)

Waller sends out his emissaries to the parts adjoining to inform the people that he had given a notable defeat to the Prince's army and broken the whole body of their force.
(Mercurius Aulicus, 9 July, 1643)

The Houses [of Parliament] *this day appointed £5000 to be sent down to Sir William Waller to be given as a largesse to his soldiers for the good service they have done.*
(A Perfect Diurnall, 10-17 July 1643)

Royalist Claims

The rebels' foot were absolutely routed and all dispersed or cut off, his loss of officers and horse very great...We are confident we killed many hundred of his men, having the field, arms, pillage and all other signs of an absolute victory.
(Mercurius Aulicus, 9 July, 1643)

At the Council of War that night were Prince Maurice, the Lord Hopton, Sir James Hamilton, Major Thomas Sheldon and some others; the result of that council was that if any of the enemy fall upon us, every man [was] *to shift for himself: in order to* [expedite] *which the cannon were drawn off: so that this battle was so hard fought on both sides, that they forsook the field first and we had leave to do so.*
(Richard Atkyns, royalist cavalry captain)

It is interesting that Atkyns did not claim outright victory for the royalists, who were themselves ready to run for it if Waller had attacked during the night. **Royalist historians**, on the other hand, have long since counted this as a royalist triumph, blinded perhaps by the undoubted bravery of the Cornish infantry in successfully storming the ridge. The fine monument raised in 1720 to the memory of Sir Bevil's courageous stand has helped to perpetuate that judgment.

Edward Hyde, Earl of Clarendon (1637-71). Close adviser to the king, but a forthright critic of the royalists' tactics at Lansdown. (Author's collection)

A more balanced view, however, would point out that although the royalists had succeeded in gaining their immediate objective (the ridge), they had completely failed to secure their strategic objective (the city of Bath). Furthermore, the storming of the ridge - one of the most reckless acts in the whole war - had helped to ensure that total victory at Lansdown would not be theirs. For it was during that action that their cavalry was lost to desertion, their infantry badly mauled, their ammunition spent and their beloved leader (Grenvile) mortally wounded. Serious doubts are therefore raised about the competency of the royalist high command in allowing the Cornish infantry to dictate tactics as they waited at the bottom of Tog Hill (see also the Earl of Clarendon's scathing criticism of this on pages 44-45).

Waller, on the other hand, was always in total control of his own army and the general situation. By choosing his fighting conditions carefully, by using long-range tactics where possible, by rapid movements under the cover of darkness and by making the most of his resources in Bath, Waller constantly outwitted the enemy. By retaining the high ground throughout, his seemingly unbalanced force had halted and turned Hopton's all-conquering Cornish army.

Lansdown was certainly **not a decisive, clear-cut victory** for either side (unlike, for example, the Battles of Marston Moor and Naseby). It is interesting to note that Waller himself, in a despatch to the Speaker of the Commons, was satisfied to suggest a draw: *We had a weary and dangerous day's fight, the night parting us; and so well did we knock each other that in the night we both retreated.* However, as the weary troops moved on to their next confrontation at Roundway Down, there is little doubt that Waller enjoyed a greater feeling of satisfaction. Furthermore, his army - refreshed and reinforced - was now in hot pursuit as they royalists limped their way to Devizes.

14

The Lansdown Campaign: Phase IV

The Sequel

Explosion on Tog Hill

Sure enough, early next morning - as Waller had predicted - the royalists admitted their brittle and exhausted condition by aborting their mission to capture Bath and withdrawing instead to Marshfield. The author of *Mercurius Aulicus* confessed that their troops by that stage were 'much tired with extreme labour and pained with hunger'. Before leaving Lansdown in the early dawn, however, royalist soldiers - following normal practice - were sent out to plunder the battlefield of armour, weapons and valuables from the bodies of the dead and dying.

To their astonishment, as some of the officers were riding about the field, they discovered (according to Hopton) three or four hundred weapons and nine or ten barrels of powder, which Waller had inadvertently left behind in the darkness. This welcome haul was loaded up onto carts and taken back to Tog Hill, where - at about 8 o'clock in the morning - a general rendezvous was called of all remaining troops prior to their march to Marshfield. Sadly, their joy at capturing the enemy's powder (for they had almost exhausted their own stocks) was short-lived. In a most terrible explosion, the powder was blown up and Sir Ralph Hopton seriously injured. Captain Richard Atkyns describes what happened just at the very moment when he and Major Sheldon had just finished speaking to Hopton:

[Sir Ralph Hopton] was then viewing the prisoners taken, some of which were carried upon a cart wherein was our ammunition; and (as I heard) had match to light their tobacco; the major desired me to go back to my regiment. I had no sooner turned my horse, and was gone three horses' lengths from him, but the ammunition was blown up and the prisoners in the cart with it; together with the Lord Hopton, Major Sheldon and Cornet Washnage, who was near the cart on horseback, and several others. It made a very noise, and darkened the air for time, and the hurt men made lamentable screeches. As soon as the air was clear, I went to see what the matter was; there I found his Lordship miserably burnt, his horse singed like parched leather, and Thomas Sheldon (that was a horse's length further from the blast) complaining that the fire was got within his

*breeches, which I tore off as soon as I could, and from as long a flaxen head of
hair as ever I saw, in the twinkling of an eye, his head was like that of a
blackamoor. His horse was hurt and run away like mad, so that I had to put him
upon my horse and get two troopers to hold him up on both sides and bring him
to the headquarters.*

The sight of Hopton's injuries was enough to turn over the stomachs of even the
tough royalist infantry. According the the correspondent of *A Perfect Diurnal*,
'Sir Ralph Hopton made a miserable spectacle, his head swollen as big as two
heads and his eyes near burnt out'.

The incident proved yet another shattering blow to the royalists'
plummeting morale. After Grenvile, Hopton was - in the view of the Earl of
Clarendon - *the soldiers' darling...whom people took to be the soul of the army.*
Slingsby, deeply saddened, described how the Cornish infantry 'drooped for their
Lord whom they loved, but also how they lamented 'that they had not powder
left to defend him'. He confessed that in reality only nine barrels remained -
while Clarendon underlined the point that no fewer than eighty barrels had been
used (much of it wasted) in the previous day's fighting.

Hopton, who was temporarily blinded (and, according to Clarendon, had
hardly so much life as not to be numbered with the dead), was gingerly placed on
a litter and carried to Marshfield. There, according to his own memoirs, the army

*The weary royalist army stages a rendezvous on Tog Hill after its abandonment of Lansdown.
Line drawing by Stephen Beck.*

rested for a day, mainly because he 'having been in the beginning of the battle shot through the arm and in the end of it blown up with gunpowder, was very unfit to be removed'. Although dangerously ill for a while, Hopton did live to fight another day - but not at the Battle of Roundway Down, where he was still too sick to take any active part.

Waller's Army Regroups

The parliamentarians, meanwhile, according to their original plans, had prepared themselves for another early march to the top of Lansdown. Just as they were ready to leave, information was brought of the royalist retreat which, according to John Vicars, 'frustrated our expectation of fighting with them as we intended'. Nevertheless, refreshed by their overnight stay in Bath, morale inside Waller's army was rising steadily in spite of their battle-weary state. Indeed, according to Slingsby, news of the explosion and Hopton's injuries 'encouraged the rebels and discouraged us' - a view echoed by Clarendon, who noted that Waller was now inspired to infuse 'new spirit into his men'.

This was further stimulated by the arrival from Bristol of fresh stocks of powder (about sixty barrels to supplement the six that remained after the battle) and fresh reinforcements (about 1,000 men). Additional recruits also flooded in from the countryside - undoubtedly aided by Waller's skilful propaganda. The royalist news-sheet, *Mercurius Aulicus*, bitterly described how Waller succeeded in recruiting large numbers of local people after the battle by sending his officers round the area *to inform the people that he had given a notable defeat to the Prince's army and broken the whole body of his force - and therefore if they would now cheerfully come in and show their zeal...by joining him in pursuit of so great a victory, they might soon make an end of the cavaliers and conclude the war.*

The willing response of the country people to Waller's summons confirms the fact that North-East Somerset was solidly parliamentarian at heart. Alexander Popham's Bath Regiment, of course, had been involved throughout the campaign - even though it had only been released by the Bristol garrison on the day of the actual battle. Similarly the general populace had given active support to the troops on Lansdown (according to compensation claims submitted by parishes at the end of the war) by despatching wagons full of supplies from such villages as Compton Dando, Whitchurch, Chelworth, Charlton ('three hundred weight of cheese') Farnborough and Thrubwell.

Furthermore, it was abundantly apparent to Slingsby that 'the country people', seeing Waller pursue the retreating royalists, began to turn against Hopton's men so that they 'could get neither meal nor intelligence, two necessary things for an army'. According to *A True Relation*, royalist soldiers, fleeing during the night after the battle, were 'taken up by the country people and brought into us'. Waller quickly adopted the normal practice of making the prisoners promise on oath not to take up arms against parliament again - and then let them 'return to their dwellings'. It was much too costly and inconvenient to keep large numbers of prisoners.

Waller, the Good Samaritan

Bath Abbey - along with the other churches - was used as a barracks, a hospital and a prison, where Waller interviewed royalist detainees. Line drawing by Stephen Back.

Meanwhile, on Thursday morning (the day after the battle), the narrow streets of Bath were crowded with soldiers, many of them maimed or showing the scars of battle. The smell of war and the stench of human excrement hovered over the city. Debris left by thousands of soldiers littered the streets, which were crowded with men and horses. Excited local citizens clustered around troops to hear the gory details of the previous day's fighting. Human compassion was given a new lease of life with wounded soldiers from both sides being provided with bread and milk by courtesy of the local council, which also donated straw for their comfort as they lay on floors inside the city's churches. Messengers clattered through the North Gate bringing news of the latest movements of the royalist army.

While a detachment of his dragoons went up to Lansdown to check the battlefield, Sir William Waller worked his way amongst this bustling throng in search of royalist prisoners. In one of the inns, he found a cavalry lieutenant, Thomas Sandys, who described how he had surrendered to a Scotsman in Waller's army. Then, according to Richard Atkyns, the Scotsman *shot him into the body with two bullets, which were still in him, so that he was very near death.* Hearing this, Waller was 'exceedingly angry' that one of his own soldiers could breach the etiquette of war in such an inhumane manner. *He sent for his own surgeon immediately,* wrote Atkyns, *and saw his wounds dressed before he went away; he gave the innkeeper charge that he should have whatever he called for, and would see him paid; that whatsoever women he sent for to attend him, should be admitted; and lent him ten broad pieces [of silver] for his own private expenses.*

But the story of Waller, the Good Samaritan, did not end there. When, several days later (after his disastrous defeat at the Battle of Roundway Down), Waller was fleeing for his own life to the safety of the Bristol garrison, he actually took time to stop in Bath to see if Sandys had recovered. Realising that the man was still too weak to accompany him as his prisoner, Waller accepted his promise that, 'when he was able to ride', he would 'render himself a true prisoner to him at Bristol'.

Shortly afterwards, following the arrival of the royalist army in Bath to claim the city, Sandys insisted that he should be allowed to honour his sworn oath to Waller. Both Atkyns and the Earl of Carnarvon tried their best to persuade him that, as he had now been freed by his own side, the promise had been rendered invalid. When Sandys continued to protest, they even put him under arrest to prevent him from carrying out his intention. The situation was finally resolved when Bristol fell to the royalists with unexpected speed and Waller fled to London. Such were the courtesies of war in the seventeenth century. Humanity and brutality were indeed close bedfellows.

Pursuit of the Royalists to Devizes

The parliamentarians did not tarry in Bath. On Friday 7 July (two days after the battle), Waller led the whole of his force - including Popham's Bath regiment - in pursuit of the enemy. The enemy was constantly harried first at Marshfield and then as it retreated through Chippenham and on to Devizes. But it was actually on Roundway Down, overlooking that town, that the fortunes of war were suddenly reversed in what emerged as a cavalry battle. Eight days after their success at Lansdown, Waller's much-vaunted cavalry (including Haselrig's Lobsters) was totally routed by fresh royalist horse regiments sent by the king from Oxford. Once Waller's cavalry had fled the battlefield, his infantry (including Popham's Bath Regiment) was surrounded and mercilessly broken.

As a result of this victory, the royalist army was able to make its way back into Somerset largely unopposed. With the ensuing fall in quick succession of Bath, Bristol and all other major garrisons (except Gloucester), the king was able to exercise control over the west country for the next two years.

Waller's dragoons return to Bath after checking the Lansdown battlefield.
Line drawing by Stephen Beck.

15

Counting the Human Cost

(a) How Many Casualties?

Throughout history, it has always been extremely difficult to calculate with any degree of accuracy the number of casualties sustained in a particular battle or war. Victors and vanquished alike inevitably put a spin on the numbers involved in an attempt to exaggerate their success or disguise their failure. The Battle of Lansdown proved no exception. Furthermore, local circumstances could make the task of providing estimates almost impossible. The dead, for instance, were sometimes buried hastily in large pits unseen by the enemy or neutral observers.

To obtain some understanding of the problem, let us examine the following contemporary accounts of what happened at Lansdown and then try to answer these questions:

> *(1) Did the royalists bury their dead in the locality, cart them away or leave them for local people to deal with?*
> *(2) How many were killed on each side?*
> *(3) What happened to the wounded?*

We shall discover that the situation is far from clear and the evidence somewhat contradictory.

Richard Atkyns (royalist)

The enemy, having intelligence of this disaster [i.e. the explosion on Tog Hill] *and also a recruit* [i.e. reinforcements] *that night of fresh men, gave us no time to repair our losses; but marched up to our headquarters* [on Tog Hill] *before we could bury our dead or make provision to secure our wounded; these (which were many) were provided for either in the Marquis's coach or litters made with boards - except Major Thomas Sheldon, who was left to the mercy of the enemy; which he perceiving, made shift to get to the rendezvous, but when he found there was nothing but a cart provided for him, what with the cold he took...he immediately died.*

The Mayor of Bristol (parliamentarian)

For they lost Sir Bevil Grenvile, Lieutenant-Colonel Joseph Ward, Sergeant-Major George Lower, Captain Bassett, Captain Cornisham, Captain James and five captains more with powder. Of ordinary men, we know not the number: seven cartloads of dead men were carried from the place - and divers wounded, twenty in a house and not one like to live; and more in other places. They lacked surgeons much. Our dead being viewed, we cannot yet find lost above fifteen, whereof only one man of note.

Mercurius Aulicus (royalist news-sheet)

Of common soldiers so few [casualties] *as 'tis not credible in so long and disadvantageous a battle as this was.*

A Perfect Diurnal (parliamentarian news-sheet)

The Lord Moon, his foot shot off with a cannon ball; what number of common soldiers the loss is not of any certainty known, in regard they [i.e. the royalists] *buried their dead.*

A True Relation (parliamentarian news-sheet)

Estimated that the royalists suffered over 200 slain and 300 wounded, whereas the parliamentarians had only 19 dead and 60 wounded (of whom four subsequently died of their injuries).

Sir William Waller's Letter to the Speaker of the Commons

Many of their chief commanders were slain or hurt; we lost only one sergeant-major of the dragoons and two cornets and not twenty common soldiers.

A Spy working for Sir Samuel Luke (parliamentarian governor of Newport Pagnell)

He reported that in late July 1643 *thirty cartloads full of maimed soldiers came into Oxford from Prince Rupert out of the west* [presumably after the Lansdown and Roundway Down campaigns]. It was common practice for commanders, where possible, to send their wounded to one of the hospitals which had been established in various towns. Oxford, of course, was the king's headquarters at the time.

John Vicars

Colonel Burghill *had received a shot through his right arm, just as his sword was even at the throat of the Lord of Carnarvon, who at this terrible conflict was also shot in the leg.*
Sir Arthur Haselrig *received a wound in his thigh with push of a pike, and after that another in his arm.*

The Earl of Clarendon

Very many officers and persons of quality were hurt - the Lord Arundel of Wardour shot in the thigh with a brace of bullets; Sir Ralph Hopton shot through the arm with a musket; Sir George Vaughan and many others hurt in the head of their troops with swords and pole-axes.

Research by Brigadier Peter Young found that sixteen royalist officers in all had been killed in the battle and a further four wounded. In addition (according to the parliamentarian news-sheet *A Weekly Account, 3-10 July 1643*), 5 officers, 97 common soldiers and 140 horses had been captured by Waller. It is hardly surprising that casualties on the royalists side were greater. They were after all far more exposed to enemy fire as they advanced from Freezing Hill over difficult and open terrain - whereas the parliamentarians were protected by their earthwork defences and later by the wall.

(d) What Cost to Local People?

During the two weeks before the Battle of Lansdown, Sir William Waller based his whole army on Bathampton and Claverton Downs in order to monitor any possible advance of the royalist force along the Avon valley. In consequence - with over 4,000 troops and 2,500 horses to accommodate and feed - inhabitants of nearby villages suffered greatly with requisitions, plunder, billeting (or 'free quarter', as it was called) and damage to crops.

The village of Combe Hay, which was nominated as the daily rendezvous point for the whole army, suffered more than most. Other local communities, however, did not escape - as demonstrated by the compensation claims (below) submitted later by parish officials for losses sustained during this episode. Newton St Loe, Norton St Phillip, Hinton Charterhouse and Charlecombe (which was dangerously near to the battlefield) all fall into this category.

Newton St Loe
....5 loads of hay for Sir William Waller's troopers, 2 for Sir Arthur Haselrig's troopers, 1 for Mr John Ashe's own horse..£5.0.0

Combe Hay
....Captain Sanderson one troop of horse and men in number 60 [for] 2 weeks and odd days, constantly quartered beside the daily concourse of the whole army to our village during Sir William Waller's being about Bath Downs and Odd Down..£42.0.0
....The same time his keeping centre on the Bath Downs, spoiling our ground ready for mowing, besides hay carried to the country to them, with exceeding spoil and loss of sheep to the number of 80...£60.0.0

Norton St Phillip
....Quartered Col. Alexander Popham's regiment of foot two days and two nights being 700 of them...£35.0.0
....Paid to Sir William Waller's quartermaster general for hay and oats when they quartered at Bradford...£06.0.0
....2 horses set forth to Sir William Waller for the use of the state to carry ammunition from Bath and never returned..£08.0.0

Charlecombe
....Sustained loss by Sir William Waller's army at the fight at Lansdown in hay, grass and wood to the value of..£10.0.0
....William Maynard's bill for bread, beer, hay and grass that was taken from him for the use of Sir William Waller when he fought at Lansdown...£05.5.6
....For bread, beer, barley, malt and other necessities taken for the use of Sir William Waller and for quartering 5 troops..£09.9.6

After the battle, the whole of Waller's army poured back into Bath for refreshment, sustenance and shelter. The city treasurer's accounts show that piles of debris were later left behind in the streets - not to mention a number of dead horses that had to be dragged out of the water courses. The Abbey and other churches were taken over as hospitals and prisons (as were the inns) with straw scattered over the floor to ease the discomfort of the wounded. Milk, bread and cheese were provided as sustenance for the sick at the council's expense. During a period of several weeks, private houses were crammed with troops from the Bath garrison, which had been established to ensure that the city was capable of withstanding any possible royalist attack. Happily the city was spared any bombardment by cannon and therefore escaped all serious damage to its fabric.

The horrors of billeting or 'free quarter' as depicted in this line drawing by Stephen Beck.

Soldiers plunder a local farm by seizing a horse, a barrel of ale and other goods.
Line drawing by Stephen Beck.

16

Archaeological Discovery and Local Legend

The Skirmishes at Monkton Farleigh and Claverton

The sensational story of the bloody skirmish on the slopes below Monkton Farleigh (see Chapter 8), which must have shattered the normally peaceful lives of local villagers, was clearly passed down through families. By the nineteenth century, **the Bathford Revels** were being held annually near the scene of the ambush in memory of a great battle fought there in times past - and stories circulated of large quantities of bones being unearthed (allegedly from mass graves) in quarrying operations nearby.

The earthworks (about one hundred metres in length), dug by Waller's men to protect the temporary bridge over the river, can still be seen in **Ham Meadow** to this day. The fierce nature of the fighting is confirmed by this rather gruesome entry in the parish registers of Claverton church:

There were buried this day under the west wall of the churchyard, three soldiers of the parliamentary party and one of the royalist party in an unhappy civil war at the riverside in the Ham Meadow at Claverton.

Over a hundred years later, the skeletons of these soldiers, identified by remains of their military clothing, were found in the churchyard when Ralph Allen's tomb was being excavated in 1764.

Further down the road on **Bathampton Meadow**, three more skeletons of civil war

The line of Waller's earthworks in Ham Meadow is still clearly visible today - earthworks which protected the river crossing. (Author's collection)

soldiers were discovered in the nineteenth century when the Great Western Railway was being built. Embedded in the chest of one of them was a 1.5 pound cannon ball.

Claverton and the Stray Cannon Ball

Another cannon ball features in a colourful and persuasive story that has been passed down through the centuries. This particular shot was allegedly fired at the manor house during the Civil War. Having crashed through the front wall of the building, it then embedded itself in the fireplace of the dining room while Sir William Bassett was actually eating at table.

The cannon ball, which is now mounted on a carved lion. (Author's collection)

There is indeed compelling evidence that such a cannon ball struck the house in the manner described. The Skrine family of Warleigh had first acquired Claverton Manor in 1714 (before its later purchase by Ralph Allen) but subsequently regained ownership in 1869. A descendent of that family, Dr Ruth Skrine, showed the author the actual cannon ball, which had come into the family's possession when the manor house was demolished in 1823. It had been mounted on a beautifully-carved lion which had stood proudly at the bottom of the building's Jacobean staircase (see left).

The story, which has probably been embellished over the years (one version even has King Charles I at table with Sir William), probably originates from the time of the 1643 skirmish. We know that the royalist army was equipped with eighteen cannons. It is more than likely, therefore, that a few shots were aimed either at Waller's army up on the downs or at the temporary bridge and earthworks in Ham Meadow - but not at the house itself (Sir William was a royalist sympathizer after all). However, such was the inaccuracy of cannon fire, it is highly probable that this particular ball landed on the manor house by mistake!

The Royalist Camp on Batheaston Meadow

The meadow site, where the royalist army camped overnight on Monday 3 July 1643, became the scene of an archaeological rescue dig during the building of the

Batheaston by-pass in 1996. The excavation, which took place at Stables Field in Kensington Meadow, unearthed a large amount of mid-seventeenth century material. This included an impressive haul of clay pipes, buttons, oyster shells and pottery fragments together with three musket bullets and a James I silver coin dated 1605. Furthermore, associated with these finds was a ditch measuring 1.65 metres wide and 0.5 metres deep - possibly a quickly-dug defensive ditch to protect the extreme edge of their camp site.

The Lansdown Battlefield Site

Artifacts relating to the battle have frequently surfaced over the years. In the nineteenth century, finds of civil war armour were reported locally as evidence that substantial burials had taken place on the site. In the later twentieth century, according to local residents, stalls at a regular antiques fair in Bath often displayed cannon balls and other such items for sale. Furthermore, at the end of a lecture on the battle, the author himself was approached by an elderly gentleman claiming that - as a boy - his class had been taken by the schoolmaster to visit a farmer who had shown them a large collection of such finds.

Finds from the Lansdown battlefield - (above) the sword; (below) the cannon ball. (Author's collection)

A few years ago, three of the author's own acquaintances - quite separately - came across exciting discoveries. One man was walking the actual slopes over which the battle was fought, when his dog unearthed a sword of the period which had been buried in an upright position (see right). The second was using a metal detector (with the farmer's permission) in the Freezing Hill/lower Tog Hill area when he located a three-and-a-half pound cannon ball (see right). This had clearly been fired from Waller's

earthworks at the advancing enemy by a minion cannon (a light field gun, which had a maximum range of around 1280 metres). The third (also using a metal detector) located a sizeable haul of musket bullets, small cannon balls, metal shoe buckles and other seventeenth-century material (see below).

When Tracy Park Golf Club was building its second course, contractors - in constructing a bunker - unearthed a store of musket bullets. This discovery provided clear reminder that skirmishing around the battlefield itself took place over a wide area. This fact was further confirmed when the author was conducting a party of schoolboys around the battlefield site. One sharp-eyed youngster actually spotted a musket bullet that had been firmly lodged in one of the dry-stone walls which surround the field which witnessed the final stage of the battler..

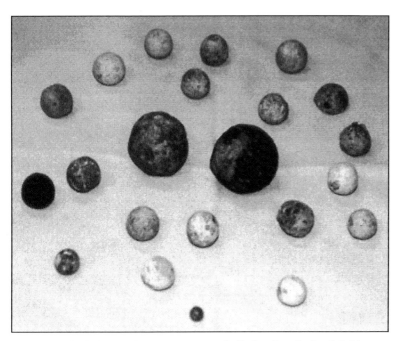

Musket bullets and miniature cannon balls found on the battlefield.
(Author's collection)

Other Stories and Legends

We know that much blood was shed on Lansdown and that the dead and dying were taken to nearby farmhouses - a drummer boy, for instance, to Goudie's Farm (just east of the battlefield) and Sir Bevil Grenvile to the Rectory at Cold Ashton, where he allegedly died sitting in a chair in the dining room. The location of that chair, which was for many years proudly shown to visitors, is no longer known.

Local legend also claims that the ghost of Grenvile still walks there to this very day; that the sound of galloping horses and the clanking of the chains on gun carriages can be heard at night on the Lansdown slopes on the anniversary of the battle; and that the brook in the village of Larkhall, fed by streams flowing off Lansdown, ran red with blood for days after the conflict. Furthermore, in the early 1990s, the author was contacted by men, who had been working during the night in buildings near the site - men who knew nothing of the battle, but who were deeply concerned at the 'strange sensations' and 'inexplicable happenings' that had been experienced.

17

The Grenvile Monument

Note: Although Sir Bevil spelt his surname as 'Grenvile', his eldest son (John) changed the spelling to 'Granville' on becoming Earl of Bath. Other members of the family eventually adopted the same style.

The monument on the Lansdown battlefield was erected in 1720 by George Granville, Lord Lansdown, in memory of his grandfather [he was the eldest son of Sir Bevil's second son, Bernard Grenvile]. There is little doubt that it was erected on the very spot where Sir Bevil fell mortally wounded, an incident which was still within the family's living memory. Sir Bevil's eldest son, John, was of course on the battlefield at his father's side when he was pole-axed.

Nevertheless, local tradition has handed down another theory about how the exact location of Grenvile's fall was confirmed. According to the Reverend Richard Warner, writing in 1801,

The actual spot was ascertained by a girl who passed the field of battle on the ensuing morning, and discovered and gave notice of it to the royal party. A very respectable gentleman in this city (who favoured me with the anecdote) had frequent conversations with the above-mentioned person, who died at the advanced age of 107; she used to say she recollected the battle extremely well, being (according to her own expression) at that time 'a hard girl ".

There is of course little doubt that local villagers would have tried to get a good view of what was happening on the battlefield from a safe distance - and then to talk to royalist soldiers afterwards (including any of the wounded who were billeted with them).

The striking monument not only displays the griffin (the family's emblem) on top, but also various other emblems on the two sides of the pedestal to commemorate the family's achievements. The east side is intended to depict the Restoration of Charles II in 1660 with the arms of England resting on the joint arms of the Duke of Albemarle and the Earl of Bath [i.e. John Grenvile, who had been lifted onto his father's horse when Sir Bevil was mortally wounded]. The west side portrays the military successes of Lord Lansdown in Hungary; while the front of the monument or south side carries the Grenvile arms borne on a Roman eagle and a tribute by the Earl of Clarendon. On the rear or north side of the pedestal is the following verse written by William Cartwright in 1643, which recalls the death of Sir Bevil, together with another one by Martin Llewellen:

His courage work'd like flames, cast heat about,
Here, there, on this, on that side none gave out,
Not any pike, in that renowned stand,
But took new force from his inspiring hand;
Soldier encourag'd soldier, man urg'd man.
And he urg'd all; so far example can.
Hurt upon hurt, wound upon wound did fall,
He was the butt, the hurt, the aim of all.
His soul this while retir'd from cell to cell,
At last flew up from all, and then he fell.
But the devot'd stand, engag'd the more
From that his fate, plied hotter than before,
And proud to fall with him, swore not to yield,
Each sought an honour'd grave, and gained the field.
Thus he being fall'n, his actions fought anew,
And the dead conquer'd whilst the living flew.

Lord Lansdown, who was elderly by the time the monument was built, was only able to supervise the operation from afar. When therefore his brother,

Colonel Bernard Granville, visited Bath for health reasons in early 1723, Lansdown seized the opportunity to gain a first-hand description of the newly-erected monument. He was, however, furious when he inspected the drawing that his brother had sent. He wrote back in indignant tones, stating that the architect had clearly ignored two crucial instructions:

> *His directions were to be sure of making the tables for the inscriptions so large that the letters might be easily legible at a distance by any passenger on horseback, and the size of the tables would be a direction to proportion the rest of the work*
>
> *It was likewise foreseen that, unless it was surrounded by a rail, it would be impossible to hinder it from being defaced by comers and goers, who would be apt to scratch their own conceits and sentences upon it; besides, cattle, which are constantly grazing upon the downs, would be rubbing against it...Therefore it was concluded there should be a handrail of stone, of which there is great plenty in all that neighbourhood and the best in the kingdom....*

Quoted in 'The Autobiography & Correspondence of Mary Granville, Mrs Delany' (1862)

His fears were well-founded. The pedestal proved far too tempting a target for the writers of graffiti. Visitors to the site today will doubtless be able to spot the earliest example dated 1722 (just two years after its erection).

The monument was subsequently restored on several occasions, including 1777 (by Bernard Calwick), 1827 and the mid-1990s (by English Heritage). R.E.M. Peach in his *Street-Lore of Bath* (1893) expressed outrage that the architect of the 1827 restoration (Edward Davis) had apparently removed the emblems from the east and west sides of the monument and erected them on an outside wall of one of the five new houses he was supervising on the southern slopes of Bath. Sure enough, the emblems there have survived to this day [although the house is private with no public access] - but the full story behind their removal remains unclear. The most likely explanation is that they were in poor condition and were therefore replaced on the monument by replicas - as can be seen today.

At least Lord Lansdown eventually gained one of his wishes for the monument is now protected against graffiti by a sizeable rail.

18

Exploring the Battle Area

Please note that the recommended map for exploration of the battle area is **Explorer 155**. Extreme care should be taken throughout - some of the lanes are extremely narrow and are often busy with traffic. Please keep to authorised paths at all times and ensure that dry stone walls are only crossed at the stiles provided.

Claverton

If driving out of Bath, take the A36 Warminster Road for about three miles, before turning right into the small village of Claverton (map reference ST 788642).

The manor house, which existed in Claverton at the time of the Civil War, was built by Sir Edward Hungerford in 1580. Its handsome appearance can be appreciated by examining below the fine drawing made by S H Grimm in 1790

Claverton Manor as it appeared at the time of the battle. The pierced wall, balustrade and stone steps of this Elizabethan building are still visible today. (By permission of the British Library).

before its demolition in 1823, following the building of a new manor above the village (now the American Museum). By the time of the skirmishes around Claverton in 1643, the manor house was in the possession of Sir William Bassett, MP for Bath and a supporter of the king.

Although the house no longer exists, it is still possible to see the pierced wall, balustrade and stone steps of the Elizabethan building. At the small church of St Mary's next door (largely 15th century and Early English in style), a number of features are worth exploring - a rainwater pipette above the south porch, which displays the Bassett arms, dated 1628; a splendid effigy of Sir William Bassett (father of the Sir William featured in our story) on the north wall of the sanctuary; a headstone commemorating Humphrey Chambers (puritan rector at the time of the war and supporter of parliament) on the floor of the sanctuary; and Ralph Allen's tomb in the churchyard (which displaced a Civil War grave). The view gained by Waller's army of the royalist approach on the other side of the river can be gained from the field behind the church.

After inspecting the village, walk down to the A46; carefully cross the road, canal and railway to visit Ham Meadow via Ferry lane (ST 792643). Then trace out the line of Waller's earthworks on this island in the middle of the river (see also Chapter 16).

A36

Marshfield, Tog Hill and Freezing Hill

A site visit to the narrow lanes, which climb up to Marshfield along **St Catherine's Valley**, is well worthwhile both for atmosphere and for gaining an understanding of the difficulties faced by the royalist army.

Driving from Bath along the A4 towards Chippenham, turn left in the village of Batheaston (signposted Northend and St Catherine). Just beyond Northend, bear left past St Catherine's Court to reach Marshfield by twisting lanes (unsignposted) - the very lanes used by the Hopton's retreating force (see right). It is best at this stage to consult the map, Explorer 155, to decide on your route, but take care - the lanes are narrow and the gradients steep at times.

In **Marshfield** itself, notice the seventeenth-century almshouses (built in 1612) at the end of the village and several Tudor and Stuart building with gables and mullioned windows. The Church of St Mary the Virgin, largely rebuilt in 1470, contains a Jacobean pulpit.

From Marshfield, drive along the A420 Bristol Road for just over a mile before turning left into **Cold Ashton** to view the outside of the Old Rectory where Sir Bevil Grenvile died (ST 752726) - see picture in Chapter 11. The house itself is private.

Then rejoin the A420. In just under a mile after the junction with the A46, turn left into Freezinghill Lane. You are now on **Tog Hill** (ST 733727). The 'cornfield', where the royalist army drew up, is on your left with the Lansdown ridge visible one-and-a-half miles away. Drive slowly down the lane to capture the atmosphere of the royalist advance (the lane and the high hedge lines are little changed since 1643) - but it is narrow and busy with no stopping places. Take note of its steepness as it drops down onto **Freezing Hill** and into the valley bottom - and then as it rises sharply onto the northern ridge of Lansdown. This will give a good impression of the problems faced by the royalists as they stormed Waller's earthworks high above them.

Just beyond the brow of the hill, park on the rough verge on the left near the monument.

The Battlefield

There are two recommended walks which enable visitors to explore the battlefield. It is always essential to wear strong walking shoes (for it is often muddy underfoot) and warm clothing at most times in the year (for it can be cool and breezy on Lansdown even in summer!). A walking stick is also useful, particularly on Walk Two. The shorter, easier walk, which lasts about 1.5 hours, takes in all the crucial areas of the battle and the features which played a prominent part in the action.

The longer walk, which lasts up to three hours, involves steep climbs and descents. It is particularly good for appreciating the difficulties of the terrain - and, if the weather is sunny, it is a beautiful walk in its own right. The routes of these walks are shown below and on the laminated map inside the back cover, which can be taken out on the exploration.

On the walks you will notice the **orange banners**, which mark out the battlefield area, and the four **interpretation panels**, which were erected at key points in 2003. You will also notice on Hanging Hill and in the area around the monument the line of **old sunken roads** or 'hollow ways'. In the seventeenth century, local people would need a number of tracks to choose from when climbing such a steep hill as this with their carts and horses. The tracks, which were of course not properly surfaced, were quickly churned up during rainy weather and soon made impassible.

WALK ONE (the numbers refer to points on the map)

1. From the parking spot, cross the road and follow the line of the Cotswold Way, passing Beach Wood on the right. [The path is actually situated inside the fence and not along the tarmac road.]

2. Notice ahead of you the Avon & Somerset Fire and Rescue HQ, which contains one of the old Cold War bunkers established in 1950 to give early warning of air and missile attacks. The path follows the orange banners before emerging onto Hanging Hill.

3. Cross the top of the field to the far corner where you will find the first of the interpretation panels. This marks the actual start of the walk. From here you get a wonderful view of both Tog Hill and Freezing Hill (and therefore the line of the royalist advance) - not to mention the steepness of the climb that faced Hopton's men. This view gives a striking impression of the extent of the battlefield and the part played by the terrain. Behind you is the flat top of Lansdown on which Waller had placed his reserves of cavalry in order to cover any attempt by the royalists to outflank his defensive line.

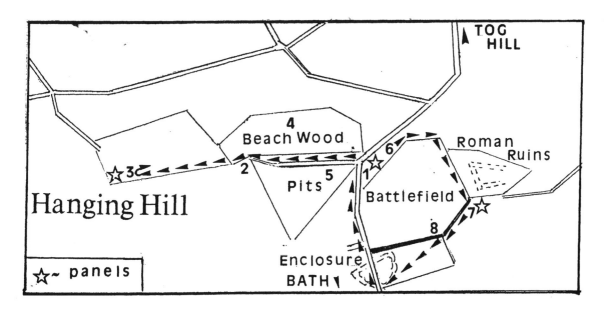

4. Now retrace your steps along the Cotswold Way, past the Fire & Rescue HQ and along the side of Beach Wood. It was somewhere here - on the edge of the wood, which marked the edge of the down's northern ridge - that Waller drew up his defensive line. We know from documentary evidence that Waller threw up temporary earthworks during the night of Tuesday 4 July on 'the brow of the hill' to provide cover for his musketeers and that some of these were placed 'in a thick wood upon the declining of the hill'.

5. Now look over to your right and notice the large number of pits in the field beyond the road. These are the Anglo-Saxon quarry pits (now somewhat overgrown) which were used during the latter stages of the battle to provide cover for the royalist musketeers, taking them to within firing range of 'Waller's Wall' (see number 8). The pits extend over a wide area - as you will see when you continue along the Cotswold Way and back again to the road. Cross the road carefully. Pause alongside the orange banner to examine the two interpretation panels, which will provide additional information on the battle.

6. Now walk down to the imposing monument, erected in 1720 in Sir Bevil Grenvile's memory by his grandson. For a full description of this see Chapter 17; for details of the mortal injury suffered by Sir Bevil on this very spot see Chapter 11. As you approach the monument, notice on your right one of the 'hollow ways' used at the time. There are also some possible indications of the gun emplacements which Waller would have erected for his cannons (i.e flat, triangular platforms of earth - particularly needed on sloping ground to prevent the guns running off down hill when fired). The cannons themselves would have been protected by earthworks and gabions (i.e. large wicker baskets filled with earth and stones). Then go down the slope beyond the monument as far as the fence, looking back to capture the extent of the challenge faced by the royalists as they edged ever closer to Waller's earthworks.

7. Now continue along the Cotswold Way, following the line of the orange banners, over the stile in the corner of the field beyond the monument. The path eventually veers right up a slope and into a large field. This is actually the field over which the battle was fought during the latter stages of the day (see Chapter 12). Walk along the left edge of the field until you come to a stile. As you cross the stile, pause on the top to look back at the adjacent field to your left. You can just pick out some markings there which represent the remains of the Roman pewter factory, in which Captain Richard Atkyns took cover during the night - but so shallow that his horse 'had a bullet in his neck'.

Once over the stile, turn right and inspect the fourth interpretation panel. Also look back at the steep hillsides which edge Lansdown, making outflanking attacks on Waller's position extremely difficult (especially bearing in mind the strength of his cavalry, which could quickly cover such threats). Follow the path along to a gate. Then take the diagonal path across the field in the direction of the road.

8. Pause half way to look at the wall on your right with the monument in the distance beyond. The wall is the wall behind which Waller's troops took cover in the latter stages of the battle. You gain a good impression of the range of battle at this point and the important role played by royalist musketeers in the old quarry pits. It is just possible to spot the breaches in the wall made by Waller for his cannon, which were filled in later by farmers [note; the wall itself is not on the official path]. Also notice the remains of the sheepcote on the left of the wall, which was also used for cover. Continue to the road, crossing with great care, and walk along the broad grass verge to your car.

Walk Two (the numbers refer to the numbers on the map)

1. From the parking spot, cross the road and follow the line of the Cotswold Way, with Beach Wood on the right. [The path is actually situated inside the fence and not along the tarmac road.].

2. It was somewhere here along the edge of Beach Wood (which marked the edge of the down's northern ridge) that Waller drew up his defensive line. We know from documentary evidence that Waller threw up temporary earthworks during

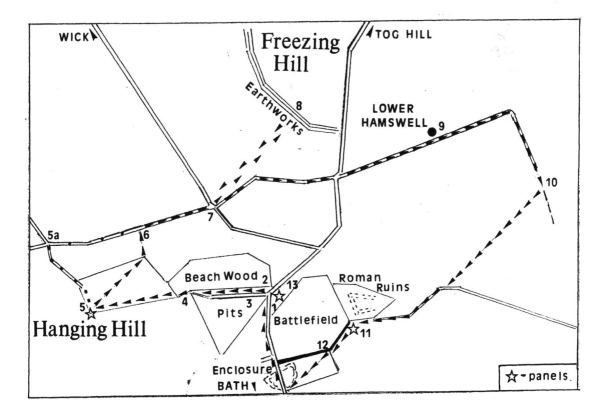

the night of Tuesday 4 July on 'the brow of the hill' to provide cover for his musketeers and that some of these were placed 'in a thick wood upon the declining of the hill'.

3. Now look over to your left and notice the large number of pits in the field beyond the road. These are the Anglo-Saxon quarry pits (now somewhat overgrown) which were used during the latter stages of the battle to provide cover for the royalist musketeers, taking them to within firing range of 'Waller's Wall' (see number 12). The pits extend over a wide area - as you will see as you continue along the Cotswold Way.

4. Notice ahead of you the Avon & Somerset Fire and Rescue HQ, which contains one of the old Cold War bunkers established in 1950 to give early warning of air and missile attacks. The path follows the orange banners before emerging onto Hanging Hill.

5. Cross the top of the field to the far corner where you will find the first of the interpretation panels. This marks the actual start of the walk. From here you get a wonderful view of both Tog Hill and Freezing Hill (and therefore the line of the royalist advance) - not to mention the steepness of the climb that faced Hopton's men. This view gives a striking impression of the extent of the battlefield and the part played by the terrain. Behind you is the flat top of Lansdown on which Waller had placed his reserves of cavalry in order to cover any attempt by the royalists to outflank his defensive line.

6. Now cross the field diagonally down hill (although the path can be indistinct in places). Aim for the farm buildings, keeping to the right of the telegraph post in the middle of the field before joining a track which leads to Beach Farm. The descent will give a good impression of the steep climb encountered by the royalists as they attacked Waller's earthworks. Note that the area still features small fields and hedges similar to those which gave cover to the royalist musketeers as they fought their way up the slopes. Then turn right along a narrow road. You are now in the bottom of the valley between Hanging Hill on your right and Freezing Hill on your left where the royalist army assembled before it launched its attack.

[6A. An interesting alternative - from the interpretation panel at no. 5, drop straight down the field in front of you (keeping about 30 metres from the left edge to avoid the shrubs). Then, in the bottom left corner, look out for a path which veers left in front of you and leads immediately to a gate bearing a footpath sign. Pass through the gate and join this 'hollow way', which royalist musketeers could well have used as they attacked Waller's flank. Its local name - Slaughter Lane - is evocative, although its actual origin is not known. Take care in following this track down to the road (no. 5A) - the track is quite steep, rocky and sometimes muddy. Turn right at the road and rejoin the the other route.]

7. On reaching the crossroads, cross with care to the stile opposite. Here you have a choice.

8. On the one hand, you can take a diversion by crossing the stile and (following the path) working your way up the steep hillside to the top of Freezing Hill, just beyond the prehistoric earthworks, where you will gain a commanding view of Waller's position on the Lansdown ridge. If you follow this option, turn right at the stile; cross the field and through a gate; then up the hill to a stile half way up the next field; then up the next field by the hedge to the earthworks. You then need to retrace your steps to number 7 on the map.

9. On the other hand, you can continue along the narrow lane to Lower Hamswell, veering right on the track at the end of the village.

10. Follow the path until, just beyond the ford, you join the Cotswold Way on your right for a steep ascent onto Lansdown. Follow the path and eventually join a track which converges from the left. This is a beautiful part of the walk with fine views on all sides.

11. The path eventually reaches one of the four interpretation panel alongside a stile. Do not cross the stile, but climb onto the top of it and look first at the field in front of you. This is actually the field over which the battle was fought during the latter stages of the day (see Chapter 12). Then look at the field to the right of the battlefield. You can just pick out some markings there which represent the remains of the Roman pewter factory, in which Captain Richard Atkyns took cover during the night - but so shallow that his horse 'had a bullet in his neck'. Now climb back down and continue along the path with a wall to your right. Also look at the steep hillsides which edge Lansdown, making outflanking attacks on Waller's position extremely difficult (especially bearing in mind the strength of his cavalry, which could quickly cover such threats).

12. Follow the path along to a gate. Then take the diagonal path across the field in the direction of the road. Pause half way to look at the wall on your right with the monument in the distance beyond. The wall is the wall behind which Waller's troops took cover in the latter stages of the battle. You gain a good impression of the range of battle at this point and the important role played by royalist musketeers in the old quarry pits. It is just possible to spot the breaches in the wall made by Waller for his cannon, which were filled in later by farmers [note; the wall itself is not on the official path]. Also notice the remains of the sheepcote on the left of the wall, which was also used for cover. Continue to the road, crossing with great care, and walk along the broad grass verge to your car.

13. Before leaving the site, however, pause alongside the orange banner to examine the two interpretation panels, which will provide additional information on the battle. Now walk down to the imposing monument, erected in 1720 in Sir

Bevil Grenvile's memory by his grandson. For a full description of this see Chapter 17; for details of the mortal injury suffered by Sir Bevil on this very spot see Chapter 11. As you approach the monument, notice on your right one of the 'hollow ways' used at the time. There are also some possible indications of the gun emplacements which Waller would have erected for his cannons (i.e flat, triangular platforms of earth - particularly needed on sloping ground to prevent the guns running off down hill when fired). The cannons themselves would have been protected by earthworks and gabions (i.e. large wicker baskets filled with earth and stones). Then go down the slope beyond the monument as far as the fence, looking back to capture the extent of the challenge faced by the royalists as they edged ever closer to Waller's earthworks. Now return to your car.

A section of 'Slaughter Lane' on the lower slopes of Hanging Hill (see page 84). Author's collection.

Who's Who in the Story

Ashe, John: a wealthy clothier from Freshford, near Bath, who employed thousands of local workers in their own homes; a devout puritan, he had opposed many of Charles I's unpopular policies before the war and had been one of the leaders of the Mendip rising in favour of parliament in July 1642 (see Chapter 4). MP for Westbury in Wiltshire, he was treasurer of parliament's Somerset committee, raising troops and money for the cause. Later, he was lukewarm over the trial of Charles I in 1649; but proposed that Cromwell should be offered the crown in 1657.

Atkyns, Captain Richard: born in Tuffley, near Gloucester, he inherited a substantial private income from his father, which he proceeded to squander. In 1643, he joined Prince Maurice's cavalry regiment in the king's own field army, seeing service in the skirmishes at Little Dean, Ripple Field and Caversham Bridge. After the regiment had been sent to reinforce the western army, he fought in the Battles of Lansdown and Roundway Down and was promoted to adjutant-general of horse. After the capture of Bristol in July 1643, he resigned his commission.

Bassett, Sir William: a barrister who owned large estates in Somerset and Cornwall; before the war, he served the local community as both a JP and a county sheriff (becoming unpopular in the process through his collection of the hated Ship Money tax). Sympathized at first with the puritan opposition to the king's policies; elected MP for Bath in 1640 and worked with the opposition until the outbreak of war in 1642, when he became at first a neutral and then a royalist sympathizer. He was subsequently disqualified from representing Bath in parliament. Inherited Claverton Manor from his father in 1613.

Burghill, Robert Colonel: had fought for the king's army as a cavalry captain in the wars in Scotland (1639-40; joined Waller's army as a major in the Civil War, distinguishing himself in the siege of Chichester and in the Forest of Dean; promoted to colonel in consequence. Fought bravely at Lansdown as commander of a cavalry regiment, but retired from service after being badly wounded in the arm in that battle.

Carnarvon, Earl of (Robert Dormer): served in the wars in Scotland (1630-40) as a colonel of horse; commanded a cavalry regiment in the royalist army at the Battles of Edgehill (1642) and Lansdown (1643), where he was shot in the leg; sent by the king with the western horse to take Dorchester, Weymouth and Portland; killed at the First Battle of Newbury (1643).

Carr, Colonel James: a Scottish professional soldier who had first been employed by the Gloucestershire committee in the defence of its county at the start of the Civil War; captured when Prince Rupert took Cirencester (February 1643), he was released in an exchange of prisoners (July); appointed by Waller as his sergeant-major-general of foot and dragoons. Fought at Lansdown; after the loss of Bristol, appointed colonel of an infantry regiment in Waller's new army (August); fought at Cheriton (1644); appointed governor of Plymouth (1644).

Dowett, Major Francis: a veteran French officer in Waller's own cavalry regiment at Lansdown; a dashing leader, he was used frequently in key manoeuvres; fought at Roundway Down. Appointed colonel of a cavalry regiment in Waller's new army (August 1643).

Grenvile, Sir Bevil: represented Cornwall or Launceston in every parliament between 1621 and 1642; at first supported the opposition to the Charles I's policies, but fought for the the king's army in the First Scots War and knighted for his services (1639); helped to raise Cornwall for the king on outbreak of the Civil War, mustering 180 of his own servants and tenants at Bodmin. Joined Hopton's army with his own infantry regiment, fighting at Braddock Down and Stratton en route to Lansdown (1643), where he was mortally wounded.

Haselrig, Sir Arthur: MP for Leicestershire (1640); a staunch puritan, he vigorously opposed the king's policies; one of the Five Members, whom Charles I tried to arrest; raised a cavalry regiment (The Lobsters) for parliament - fought at Edgehill, Lansdown, Roundway Down and Cheriton. After the war, appointed Governor of Newcastle (1647) and Governor of Berwick (1650); supported the trial of Charles I, but eventually broke with Cromwell; imprisoned at the Restoration of Charles II (1660); died in the Tower.

Hertford, Marquis of (William Seymour): member of Charles I's privy council; appointed lord lieutenant of Somerset (1639); made marquis (1640); joined the king in York, but sent to the west country as lieutenant-general of the west to raise an army (1642). Not really a soldier, but rather a scholar (Chancellor of Oxford University (1643-47); took precedence on the battlefield over Hopton etc by virtue of his title. Sent by the king from Oxford to reinforce Hopton's new Cornish army, capturing Taunton, Bridgwater and Dunster in the process. Fought at Lansdown, Roundway Down and Bristol (1643). Then recalled to court; surrendered at Oxford; but later fined by parliament for his part in the war. Died in 1660 just after the Restoration of Charles II.

Hopton, Sir Ralph: a Somerset landowner, campaigned with Waller as a volunteer in the Thirty Years' War (1620). Represented Bath, Wells and Somerset at various times (1625-42), but expelled from parliament after changing from opposition to support of the king. Raised a Cornish army - fought at Braddock Down, Stratton, Lansdown, Roundway Down (all 1643) and Cheriton (1644). Appointed Governor of Bristol and commander of the king's western army (1643). Defeated at Torrington and subsequently surrendered (1646). Lived in exile in Jersey, Holland and Bruges. Died in 1652.

Maurice, Prince: a German by birth, brother of Prince Rupert; volunteered to help his uncle, Charles I, at the start of the Civil War. Lieutenant-general of horse in Hertford's army - fought at Lansdown, Roundway Down and Bristol (1643); appointed lieutenant-general of the western army (1643-44), campaigning in the south-west and later on the Welsh border. Fought at Naseby (1645). Fled abroad after the war, joining Rupert in a career of piracy on the high seas; lost at sea in a storm.

Popham, Colonel Alexander: a large landowner in Somerset, Wiltshire and Devon; a puritan, elected MP for Bath (1640); appointed commander of the Bath Regiment of Trained Bands; played a major part in raising North Somerset for parliament. Fought at Lansdown and Roundway Down (1643); appointed colonel of a cavalry regiment in Waller's new army (1643); returned to Somerset with the New Model Army (1645). After the war, supported Cromwell; during the Protectorate, made a member of the Council of State and the Second House (which replaced the Lords). After the Restoration, entertained Charles II at Littlecote House.

Slanning, Colonel Sir Nicholas: knighted (1632); Governor of Pendennis Castle (1635); fought in the king's army in the wars in Scotland (1639). At the start of the Civil War, raised a regiment of Cornish volunteers and commanded an infantry regiment in Hopton's new army; fought at Braddock Down, Stratton, Lansdown and Bristol, where he was mortally wounded (all 1643).

Waller, Sir William: Served as a volunteer with Hopton in the Thirty Years' War (1620); knighted (1622); MP for Andover (1640). Supported parliament in the Civil War, fighting at Edgehill and in the southern counties (1642); appointed major-general of parliament's western army (1643); gained control of the Severn valley; halted the royalist advance at Lansdown, but defeated at Roundway Down (1643). Appointed commander of a new southern army (1644); defeated Hopton at Cheriton, but lost at Cropredy Bridge. After the war, fell out with Cromwell and was suspected of intrigues with the royalists; imprisoned for three years (1648). Supported the Restoration. MP for Westminster (1660). Died 1665.

Bibliography

PRINTED DOCUMENTARY MATERIAL

Firth, C H (ed.): *Memoirs of Sir Edmund Luke*, 2 vols. (Oxford, 1894 edtn.)

Foster, Henry: *A True and Exact Relation of the Marching of the Trained Bands*, 1645 (in John Washbourne, *Bibliotheca Gloucestrensis*, 1825)

C E H Healey (ed.): Sir Ralph Hopton: *Bellum Civile* (in Somerset Record Society, vol. 18. 1902 - which also reproduces *Colonel Slingsby's Relation of the Battles of Lansdown and Roundway Down*)

Longmore, Sir T (ed.): *Richard Wiseman: Surgeon and Sergeant-Surgeon to Charles II* (1891)

Macray, W D (ed.): Earl of Clarendon, *The History of the Rebellion and the Civil War in England*, 6 vols (1912)

Philips, I G (ed.): *The Journal of Sir Samuel Luke*, vol. 1 (in Oxford Record Society, vol. 29 - 1947; vol. 31 - 1950)

Portland MSS, vol. 3: *Captain Edward Harley to Sir Robert Harley, 15 July 1643* (Historical Manuscripts Comsn)

Vicars, John: *Jehova-Jirah, God in the Mount: or England's Parliamentarie Chronicle* (1646)

Young, Peter (ed.): *The Praying Captain - A Cavalier's Memoirs* (in Journal of Historical Research, vol. 35, 1957). The memoirs of Richard Atkyns; useful appendix.

Young, Peter & Tucker, Norman (eds.): *Military Memoirs of the Civil War - Richard Atkyns and John Gwyn* (1967)

SECONDARY SOURCES

Adair, John: *Roundhead General: The Campaigns of Sir William Waller* (1997 edtn.)

Battlefields Trust Resource Centre (internet: www.battlesfieldstrust.com): *Battle of Lansdown Hill*

Carleton, Charles: *Going to the Wars: The Experience of the British Civil Wars, 1638-1651* (1992)

Donagan, Barbara: *The Casualties of War* (n.d.)

Edgar, F R T: *Sir Ralph Hopton: The King's Man in the West, 1642-52* (1968)

English Heritage: *Battlefield Report: Lansdown Hill* (1994)

Firth, C H: *Cromwell's Army* (1962 edtn.)

McCreadie, Rory: *The Barber-Surgeon's Mate of the 17th Century* (1997)

Morris, Robert: *The Battles of Lansdown & Roundway, 1643* (1993)

Peachey, Robert & Turton, Alan: *The Fall of the West, vol. 5: The Military Units - Somerset etc* (1994)

Stucley, John: *Sir Bevill Grenvile and His Times, 1596-1643* (1983)

Tucker, John & Winstock, Lewis (eds.): *The English Civil War: A Military Handbook* (1972)

Wroughton, John: *A Community at War: the Civil War in Bath and North Somerset, 1642-50* (1992)

Wroughton, John: *An Unhappy Civil War: The Experiences of Ordinary People in Gloucestershire, Somerset & Wiltshire, 1642-46* (1999)

Wroughton, John: *Stuart Bath: Life in the Forgotten City, 1603-1714* (2004)

Wroughton, John: *The Routledge Companion to the Stuart Age, 1603-1714* (2006)

ORIGINAL DOCUMENTARY MATERIAL

Bath Record Office:	Bath Chamberlain's Accounts, 1569-1662
	Bath Council Books, No. 1, 1631-49
Bodleian Library:	Tanner Mss, 62, f 164 (Waller to Speaker, 12 July 1643)
British Library:	News-sheets & pamphlets from the collection of Thomason Tracts:-

A True Relation of the Great and Glorious Victory...obtained by Sir William Waller...July 14 1643

A Copy of a Letter sent from the Mayor of Bristol to a Gentleman, 1643

A Perfect Diurnall, 10-17 July 1643

Special Passages, 12-19 July 1643

Mercurius Aulicus, 8 July 1643

INDEX